Business Planning Essentials

FOR DUMMIES®
A Wiley Brand

by Veechi Curtis

FOR DUMMIES®
A Wiley Brand

Business Planning Essentials For Dummies®

Published by
Wiley Publishing Australia Pty Ltd
42 McDougall Street
Milton, Qld 4064
www.dummies.com

Copyright © 2014 Wiley Publishing Australia Pty Ltd

The moral rights of the author have been asserted.

National Library of Australia
Cataloguing-in-Publication data:

Author:	Curtis, Veechi
Title:	Business Planning Essentials For Dummies / Veechi Curtis
ISBN:	9781118641262 (pbk.)
	9781118641293 (ebook)
Series:	For Dummies.
Notes:	Includes index.
Subjects:	Business planning.
Dewey Number:	658.4012

Cover image: © iStock.com/kaan tanman

Typeset by diacriTech, Chennai, India

Printed in Singapore by
C.O.S. Printers Pte Ltd

10 9 8 7 6 5 4 3 2 1

Contents at a Glance

Introduction *1*

Chapter 1: Letting Your Plan Take Flight 7

Chapter 2: Figuring Out What's So Special about You 19

Chapter 3: Sizing Up the Competition 27

Chapter 4: Spotting Opportunities, Dodging Threats 39

Chapter 5: Separating Yourself from Your Business 49

Chapter 6: Budgeting for Start-Up Expenses 65

Chapter 7: Figuring Out Prices and Predicting Sales 77

Chapter 8: Calculating Costs and Gross Profit 91

Chapter 9: Planning for Expenses 107

Chapter 10: Assembling Your Profit & Loss Projection 119

Chapter 11: Developing a Strong Marketing Plan 133

Chapter 12: Pulling Together Your Written Plan 147

Chapter 13: Ten (Almost!) Questions to Ask before You're Done 161

Index *167*

Table of Contents

Introduction *1*

    About This Book 1
    Foolish Assumptions 2
    Icons Used in This Book 3
    Beyond the Book..3
    Where to Go From Here 3

Chapter 1: Letting Your Plan Take Flight **7**

    Getting Your Feet Wet 8
        Deciding who this plan is for......................................8
        Choosing your dance partners.....................................8
        Looking at online planning tools.................................9
    Scoping the Nature of Your Plan 11
        Structuring your plan...11
        Setting aside enough time 12
        Deciding how far into the future you want to go...15
    Scoring Your Business...16

Chapter 2: Figuring Out What's So Special
about You **19**

    Understanding Strategic Advantage....................................20
        Looking at examples of strategic advantage 20
        Understanding how risk relates to gain 21
    Justifying Why You Can Succeed......................................22
    Developing Your Strategic Advantage Statement............24
        Drafting your statement 24
        Growing your advantages over time.......................25
    Looking Around for More Ideas..26

Chapter 3: Sizing Up the Competition **27**

    Understanding Why Analysing Competitors is So
        Important 28
    Engaging in Cloak-and-Dagger Tactics 29
        Doing a competitor profile.......................................29
        Mirror, mirror on the wall ... .31
    Choosing Your Competitive Strategy................................32
        Weighing up your options 33
        Matching competitive strategy to your strategic
        advantage..34

Taking a Bird's-Eye View 35
Thinking about future competitors........................35
Observing industry trends 36
Responding to industry trends...............................37

**Chapter 4: Spotting Opportunities,
Dodging Threats 39**

Looking at Your Strengths and Weaknesses 40
Putting yourself through the griller.........................40
Prioritising where you need to do better 41
Identifying Opportunities and Threats............................42
Pulling the Pieces Together...45
Putting theory into practice 45
Translating your SWOT analysis into action..........46

**Chapter 5: Separating Yourself from Your
Business 49**

Deciding What Path You Want to Take................................50
Doing the thing you love to do................................51
Getting help and delegating what you can 52
Building a business that's separate from you 53
Creating a way of doing business 54
Wearing Different Hats 56
Building a Business with a Life of its Own......................58
Defining your difference 58
Documenting and building systems........................60
Setting goals for you and your business.................62
Planning for a graceful exit 63
Appreciating the Limitations of Your Business................63

Chapter 6: Budgeting for Start-Up Expenses....... 65

Creating a Start-Up Budget...66
Purchasing materials and inventory.......................66
Listing your start-up expenses 67
Including expenses paid for out of
personal funds 69
Adding enough to live on 69
Separating Start-Up Expenses from Operating
Expenses 70
Assessing How Much You Really Need................................71
Understanding Finance Options 72
Getting into bed with the bank................................73
Offering up collateral 74
Seeking equity partners..74
Borrowing from family..75

Chapter 7: Figuring Out Prices and Predicting Sales 77

Choosing Pricing Strategies 78
    Setting prices based on costs..................................78
    Setting prices based on competitors......................78
    Setting prices based on perceived value 79
Building a Hybrid Pricing Plan..............................80
    Offering a premium 80
    Cutting back the frills 80
    Getting creative with packages 81
    Charging different prices for the same thing..81
Forming Your Plan of Attack.................................82
Building Your Sales Forecast.................................83
    Calculating hours in a working week......................84
    Predicting sales for a new business........................86
    Predicting sales for an established business 87
Creating Your Month-by-Month Forecast 88

Chapter 8: Calculating Costs and Gross Profit 91

Calculating the Cost of Each Sale........................92
    Identifying your variable costs................................92
    Costing your service...94
    Costing items you buy and sell 94
    Creating product costings for manufacturers........96
Understanding Gross Profit..................................97
    Calculating gross profit...97
    Figuring out gross profit margins...........................98
    Looking at margins over time...................................98
Analysing Margins for Your Business 99
    Calculating margins when you charge by the hour...99
    Calculating margins when you sell products 100
    Calculating margins if you do big projects...........101
Building Your Gross Profit Projection.................102
    Simply you..103
    Adding little helpers...103
    Small-scale productions...104
    More in the mix...105

Chapter 9: Planning for Expenses 107

Concentrating on Expenses.................................108
    Separating start-up expenses from other expenses 108

Thinking of what expenses to include...........109
Building a 12-month projection 112
Finetuning Your Worksheet 114
Recognising relationships 114
Allowing for irregular payments...............115
Playing the 10 per cent rule......................115
Thinking about Taxes and Loan Repayments...............116
Allowing for personal and company tax 116
Understanding where other taxes fit in 116
Dealing with loan repayments and interest..........117
Factoring in Personal Expenses.........................118

**Chapter 10: Assembling Your Profit &
Loss Projection 119**

Understanding More About Spreadsheets 120
Building Your Profit & Loss Projection............120
Step one: Projected sales 120
Step two: Variable costs 122
Step three: Expenses budget 123
Step four: The bottom line......................125
Step five: Tax, glorious tax....................125
Checking you've got it right....................126
Analysing Net Profit..............................127
Calculating net profit margins 127
Assessing whether your net profit is
reasonable, or not 127
Thinking further ahead..........................128
Taking Things a Step Further.....................129
Measuring risk and your comfort factor.............129
Looking at cashflow 129
Creating Balance Sheet Projections...............131

**Chapter 11: Developing a Strong
Marketing Plan 133**

Laying Down the Elements 134
Writing an eloquent introduction...............134
Building a brand people want...................135
Defining Your Target Market 136
Thinking creatively about channels...............137
Researching the market.........................137
Setting Sales Goals and Strategies..................138
Thinking beyond the dollar.....................138
Getting SMART 139
Creating strategies to support your targets.........140
Planning for Customer Service 142

Keeping Yourself Honest...................................143
    Comparing targets and actuals..............................143
    Tracking referral sources 144
    Analysing online success.......................................145

Chapter 12: Pulling Together Your Written Plan . . . 147

Reviewing the Overall Structure......................................148
Introducing Your Business 151
    Devising a mission statement...............................151
    Crafting a company description...........................152
    Refining your overall strategy 153
Plunging into the Financials...154
    Presenting your key reports 154
    Pleading for finance...155
Completing the Rest of Your Plan 156
    Selling yourself and your team............................156
    Providing a quick summary of operations 157
    Introducing the killer marketing plan..................158
Setting Milestones for Every Step 158

Chapter 13: Ten (Almost!) Questions to Ask before You're Done 161

Can You Summarise Your Business in 30 Seconds or
    Less? 161
Does Your Plan Truly Evaluate Competitors?................162
Have You Double-Checked Your Numbers? 163
Do Your Numbers Fit Your Goals?...................................163
Have You Cast Your Net as Wide as Possible? 164
Have You Made Any Assumptions You Can't Justify? ...165
What Do Others Think? 165
Do You Have a Get-Out Plan?..166
Is Your Plan Inspirational?..166

Index 167

Introduction

● ●

*W*hile working on this book, I realised something quite fundamental. Although I've been steadily successful in my own business for over 20 years, all too often the sensible-cardigan-wearing-accountant side of me wins out against the risk-taking-creative-why-don't-we-try-this side of me. Possibly due to the rather precarious finances of my childhood, I typically spend more time analysing profit margins than I do thinking of creative new products; I focus more on managing risk than being a trendsetter.

If you've been in business before, I'm sure you too have experienced this natural tension between your entrepreneurial side and the inner voice of 'reason'.

One challenge for me in writing this book has been to find ways to encourage dreams to flourish while simultaneously exploring the somewhat sobering process of writing a business plan. I'm writing this introduction having just finished the last chapter of this book, and happily, I think that the process has worked on me. I'm itching with impatience to begin my next business venture, and feel utterly optimistic about its prospects.

I hope you have a similar experience with this book, and that I share enough inspiration for your inner entrepreneur to thrive while at the same time providing unshakeable feet-on-the-ground practicality.

About This Book

I like to think that this book is a bit different from other business planning books, not least because this book is part of the *For Dummies* series. Dummies books aren't about thinking that you're a 'dummy' — far from it. What the *For Dummies* series is all about is balancing heavyweight topics with a lightweight mindset, and sharing a 'can-do' attitude that encourages anyone — no matter how young or old, how inexperienced or how veteran — to give the subject at hand a go.

I like to think that the *For Dummies* way of thinking has helped me to bring a fresh approach to the subject of business planning. I've tried not to get bogged down in the same old stodgy discussions of mission statements, values and organisational charts. Instead, I've focused more on working with others, being creative and thinking of your business as something that's unique and separate from yourself.

You may be surprised by the fact that I devote five whole chapters to the topic of finance (you'll only find one finance chapter in most business planning books). I'm a real advocate of the importance of financial planning and in this book, I try to break the topic down into bite-sized chunks that anyone can understand, even if they've never done any bookkeeping or accounting before.

I also understand that most people who've worked in business end up with knowledge that's patchy. You may know heaps about marketing but nothing about finance, or vice versa. The beauty of *For Dummies* books is that you can just leap in, find the chunk of information that addresses your query, and start reading from there.

Foolish Assumptions

When writing this book, I make no assumptions about your prior experience. Maybe you've been in business all your life or maybe you've never been in business before. It could be that you're a tech geek or it's possible that you hate computers. Maybe you love numbers or — much more likely — you may have a somewhat queasy feeling when it comes to maths.

I also make no assumptions about the age of your business, and realise that for many people reading this book, your business is still a seedling waiting to be watered. (For this reason, I include practical advice, such as how to budget for personal expenses while you're building your business, and why things such as your relationships and family situation are all part of the picture.)

Last, I don't try to guess where you live in the world. After all, the principles of business planning are universal, whether you're in the snowdrifts of Alaska, the stone country of Australia or the kilt-swaying highlands of Scotland.

Icons Used in This Book

Want to get the killer edge? Then look for this handy icon.

This icon highlights free resources, worksheets, templates and checklists you can find online at www.dummies.com/go/ businessplanningessentials.

Tie a knot in that elephant's trunk, pin an egg-timer to your shirt but, whatever you do, don't forget …

This icon points to ways to give your business plan that extra spark.

A pitfall for the unwary. Read these warnings carefully.

Beyond the Book

I've created a whole heap of Excel and Word templates to make it easier for you to create your first plan. The Excel templates provide a great starting point for most of the financial projections, while the Word templates help you structure the narrative parts of your plan. You can find all of these templates at www.dummies.com/go/businessplanningessentials.

Speaking of which, I really like to think of my books as a conversation with readers, rather than a one-way monologue. If you have any comments, questions or feedback, then I'd love to hear from you. Please feel free to email me: veechi@ veechicurtis.com.au or go to Facebook and search for **Veechi Curtis**.

Where to Go From Here

Business Planning Essentials For Dummies is no page-turning thriller (probably a good thing given the subject matter) and doesn't require you to start at the beginning and follow through to the very end. Instead, feel free to jump in and start reading the chapters most relevant to you:

- ✔ If you're new to business and you've never created a business plan before, I suggest you read Chapters 1, 2 and 3 before doing much else. Chapter 1 provides a road map for creating your plan, and Chapters 2 and 3 help you to consolidate your business concept. From here, you're probably best to read the chapters in the order that I present them, as these chapters follow the same sequence as the topics within a business plan.

- ✔ If business strategy is more your concern, then Chapters 2, 3, 4 and 5 are the place to be.

- ✔ Are financial projections a source of woe? Chapters 6 through to 10 are here to help.

- ✔ For advice on creating a marketing plan, head to Chapter 11.

- ✔ For advice on creating a plan that can't fail to impress prospective lenders or investors, Chapter 12 explains how to pull your plan together and Chapter 13 offers a handy checklist to make sure you don't forget a thing.

Five Things to Remember when Planning Your Business

- **Be prepared.** Act quickly and decisively — but not impulsively! — when opportunities arise.

- **Watch what's happening in your industry.** Monitor trends carefully and be wary of an industry in decline. Network with others and keep up to date with changes in technology.

- **Stay creative and inventive with pricing.** If possible, create different pricing structures for different kinds of customers. Experiment with premiums, discounts and packages.

- **Be pragmatic about the risks and do your sums carefully.** But at the same time, stay unshakeable in your self-belief.

- **Remember that a business is like a child.** In the end, your business needs to stand separate from you in order to flourish.

Chapter 1

Letting Your Plan Take Flight

In This Chapter

▶ Getting started without another moment's hesitation

▶ Thinking about the structure of your plan and how long it's going to take

▶ Rating yourself and your business idea with a quick and easy quiz

*Y*ou probably already know that if you spend time working *on* your business — rather than just working *in* your business — you have a much better chance of higher sales, more profit and a generally easier existence.

One of the main reasons people don't get around to creating a business plan is that they think they don't have enough time. Pish tosh. You don't need to spend weeks creating an impressive 30-page document. Instead, what you need to do is change your way of thinking. Rather than making a daily 'to do' list of all the people you have to call, brew yourself a cup of tea and have a think about your pricing strategies. Rather than fretting about all the jobs that need doing, spend a couple of hours researching your competitors.

Some of the most important elements of a business plan can be done while you're in the shower, on the beach or driving your car. Attitude is everything. To create a great business plan, all you need is a willingness to be objective about your strategy, the discipline to analyse your financials (even if you're not naturally good with numbers) and the ability to think of your business as something that's separate from you.

So no more excuses, no skipping to another chapter, no closing this book with a sigh. It's time to start planning and there's no time like the present.

Getting Your Feet Wet

Some of my best business ideas have come to me while lying in the hammock at our holiday house, digging up weeds in the garden or having a quiet coffee down at the village.

In *Business Planning Essentials For Dummies* I place less emphasis on the importance of creating a written plan and more on why planning is best viewed as an all-year-round activity. The neat thing about this way of thinking is that you can start your plan at any time, even if you know you only have one hour free this week and you're flying to Europe for a skiing holiday the next.

Deciding who this plan is for

You, of course. Your plan is an ongoing process, not a massive document that you create every year or so. Feel free to pick a structure, time and format that works well for you.

Occasionally, other people may want to have a stickybeak at your plan, usually prospective investors or lenders. On these occasions, you probably want to create a formal plan using a fairly traditional format, and focus more on the presentation and readability of your plan.

One thing to bear in mind, however: Regardless of who is likely to read your plan, I strongly suggest that when it comes to the financials — sales targets, income projections, profit projections and so on — you be consistent. Don't have one version of financials for your own purposes and another spruced-up version for the bank.

Choosing your dance partners

As a business owner, you need to have a good understanding of your financials, a solid commitment to marketing, a razor-sharp insight into your competition and a keen sense of strategy. Even if you don't have all of these skills yet, I can't think of a better way of acquiring these skills than getting involved in your own business plan. Experience is a generous teacher.

Having said this, unless you've run a business before, you'll almost certainly need a little help from outside. The good news is you simply need to ask. Consider these sources:

✔ **Business planning courses:** In my opinion, a structured course spread over several weeks or even months is the very best possible way to accumulate basic planning skills. Not only do you have the discipline of working on your plan at least once a week, but you also usually receive expert mentoring from teachers, as well as peer support from other people in a similar position to you.

✔ **Business advisory centres:** Depending on where you are in the world, business advisory centres have different names and structures. However, most state and federal governments fund some form of free advisory centres.

✔ **Business consultants:** While I warn against delegating the whole planning process to outsiders, expert consultants can be a great resource, especially if you retain control and ownership of your plan.

✔ **Your accountant:** I strongly recommend that you do your own financial projections, rather than delegating this task to a bookkeeper or accountant. (I explain just how in Chapters 6 through to 10.) However, after you've made your best attempt, consider asking your accountant to review your figures and help you to identify anything that doesn't make sense or seems unrealistic.

✔ **Your lawyer:** An important part of business planning is risk management, including protecting your name and your brand, and limiting liability through company structures. Your lawyer is an excellent source of advice for this part of the planning process.

✔ **Friends and family:** Not only is the advice of friends and family usually free, but these people also understand you like nobody else. Support and encouragement from friends and family is invaluable on those doubtful days when you think you (and your new business idea) may be crazy.

✔ **Your spouse/life partner:** Last but not least. Need I say more?

Looking at online planning tools

In *Business Planning Essentials For Dummies*, I provide you with everything you need to build your plan, including a whole bunch of free templates and resources that you can download from www.dummies.com/go/businessplanningessentials. You may be wondering how these templates compare to the many business planning templates or software applications you can find online (many of which are also free).

At a surface level, most of these templates provide you with pretty much everything you need to create a plan. However, when writing this book, I've reflected on my experience from running business plan courses. What I find is that some concepts of business planning that may take only a few sentences to summarise are really hard for those new to business to grasp.

For example, almost anyone can explain the concept of strategic advantage in a few sentences, and most business planning templates simply provide a Word template with a few blank lines in which you can write your strategic advantage. In real life, I find that these concepts usually take several sessions to gel with my students. It's for this reason that I devote two whole chapters to the concepts of strategic and competitive advantage (Chapters 2 and 3) and I recommend that you read these chapters early in your business planning process, so you can be sure a solid foundation is in place when you create your plan.

However, what you may find works well is to use a business planning template in conjunction with this book. You can dig up a whole heap of industry-specific templates online, and you may even find topics within these templates that I don't cover in detail within this book. (Bplans, at www.bplans.com is probably the world's leader in business planning templates and software and provides an excellent starting point.)

As well as business planning templates, you can also consider business-planning software. You can either buy software that you install on your computer (such as Business Plans Pro available from www.bplans.com or MAUS MasterPlan available from www.maus.com.au), or you can subscribe to online planning software in the cloud (such as www.liveplan.com or www.planhq.com). I prefer cloud-based software because you can pay as you go, and because cloud computing makes working collaboratively with others so much easier.

The main difference between business planning templates and business planning software is the sophistication of the financials. For example, the financials in most business planning software packages (including those in the cloud) include Profit & Loss Projections, Cashflow Projections, budgets, break-even analysis, Balance Sheets and more. You usually find that all the financials interconnect so that if you change a figure in your Profit & Loss Projection, the change automatically flows through to the other financial reports.

While business planning software can be a real benefit if figures and maths don't come naturally to you, the downside can be inflexibility (for example, you may find you can't adapt the list of expenses or that the format for sales projections is limited). Assuming you have a decent internet connection, why not weigh up the pros and cons for yourself by subscribing to a service such as www.liveplan.com for 30 days or so. Subscriptions cost approximately US$19.95 per month and a small payment of this nature is hardly likely to break the bank.

Scoping the Nature of Your Plan

While planning is certainly best done on an ongoing basis, the ideal approach the very first time you create a business plan is to cover all the elements of your plan — concept, strategy, financials, marketing, people and so on — within a reasonable time frame, and then collate all your workings into a single document. This approach requires a certain level of discipline, but by the time you get to the end you're going to be left with a major sense of achievement.

Structuring your plan

The best format for a business with a turnover of $100 million and 200 employees is going to be utterly different from the best format for a start-up business with no employees. For this reason, you can find as many possible formats for a business plan as recipes for bolognese sauce.

What most formats have in common, however, is certain key elements, although the sequence of these elements varies. (The following section outlines how much time each element is likely to require and also tells you where to find more detailed information on each one.)

Here are the key elements of a business plan:

- ✓ **An overview of the business and its strategy**. This introduction to your plan includes your mission, a brief description of your business and a strategic advantage statement.

✔ **A people plan**. Who are you, and why are you so awesome? What are your skills and the skills of those involved in your business?

✔ **An analysis of industry and economic trends, as well as a summary of what you perceive to be opportunities or threats**. No business is an island, particularly in a very fast-changing world. This part of your plan looks at factors outside of your control (such as industry or economic trends), possible opportunities that your business could exploit, and threats that you need to guard against.

✔ **A complete summary of financials**. At its simplest, the financial part of your plan may only include a Profit & Loss Projection for the next 12 months. More detailed plans include Profit & Loss Projections for 24 or 36 months ahead, plus historical Profit & Loss reports and Balance Sheets for the previous year or years. Financials often also include break-even analysis, Cashflow Projections and budgets.

✔ **A marketing plan**. A marketing plan is usually several pages long and includes competitor analysis, unique selling points, target market analysis, sales targets, marketing strategies and a bit more besides.

✔ **A summary of goals**. Here's where you get to share your dreams, neatly sliced and diced into monthly, six-monthly and yearly goals.

In this book, I work through the preceding six key elements in sequence. The only exception is the mission statement, which normally goes at the beginning of a business plan, which I leave until Chapter 12 to address. (From experience, I find it works best to delay writing a mission statement until further into the planning process.)

Setting aside enough time

Here's a bit more detail about how much time the different elements of a business plan (listed in the preceding section) typically require, and how often you need to attend to them.

Business model and strategy

How long does it take to come up with a decent business model? If you're lucky, you may be able to work out a winning strategy over the course of a few drinks. Alternatively, you may find it takes years to come up with a strong strategy that really works.

As well as working out a strong business strategy, the other element of developing your business model is doing a detailed analysis of your competitors. This process usually takes only a few hours, but is something that you should do every six months or so to avoid being caught by surprise.

I talk about business strategy in Chapters 2, 4 and 5, and focus on competitive analysis in Chapter 3.

Industry and SWOT analysis

The first time you do this part of your plan, which includes both an industry analysis and a SWOT (Strengths, Weaknesses, Opportunities and Threats) analysis, can take a fair chunk of time, depending on the depth in which you choose to explore this topic.

I don't usually see the need for you to update the written element of this part of your plan any more often than once a year. However, being alert to the impact of things changing around you is something you want to maintain all year round. Find ways to stay tuned to changes in your industry, possibly by attending conferences, subscribing to forum boards, researching information on industry websites or attending industry association meetings.

Planning for risk doesn't generally require significant time on an ongoing basis, but tends to demand your attention in fits and starts (for example, trademarking a logo or drawing up employee contracts may take several days to organise). However, I suggest you allow at least half a day or so each year to review your risk-management strategies.

I talk about industry and SWOT analysis in Chapters 3 and 4.

People plan

A business isn't anything without the people who run it, and your skills, entrepreneurialism and natural abilities are as much a part of the mix as anything else, as are the skills of the people you choose to involve in your business. This part of your plan needs to outline the people element of your business: Who does what, and why they're the best choice for the job.

Even if you don't have any employees yet, you can still include details about any consultants, advisers, mentors or professionals you plan to involve in your business. These details help to establish credibility for anybody else reading your plan, and prompt you to think further outside the business than just yourself.

Chapter 2 touches on this topic, while Chapter 5 explores the people side of your plan in more depth. (People planning doesn't necessarily take a huge amount of time at first, but is something that can be a huge time-waster if you don't get it right.)

Financials

Creating a Profit & Loss Projection (Chapters 7 through to 10) can be pretty time-consuming the first time around, and may take several days if you're not used to working with figures or Excel. Stick with the process, though, because your next attempt will only take a fraction of the time.

So how often do you need to review your financial plan? I recommend you compare budgets against actual results every month when you look at your Profit & Loss report. As patterns emerge (maybe you can see that you consistently over- or under-estimate something), return to your overall Profit & Loss Projections, revise your figures, and extend these projections again so they span a full 12 months ahead.

 If your business is always tight for cash and you carry high levels of stock or customer debt, you or your finance manager may need to do Cashflow Projections as well as Profit & Loss Projections, updating figures on a constant basis.

I explain how to create a Profit & Loss Projection in Chapters 7 to 10.

Marketing plan

I love doing marketing plans. Thinking about sales strategies is such a creative process that it's hard not to feel a charge of energy and inspiration as you flesh out your ideas.

Creating your first marketing plan can take anywhere from several hours to several days to nut out. After the first time, however, maintaining a coherent marketing plan generally only requires a half-day or so every six months.

I explore marketing plans in detail in Chapter 11.

An action plan

The action plan is where you weave all the other elements of your plan together into a neat summary of goals and objectives, each one with a time frame. In other words, the action plan is the section that endeavours to keep you on track, hopefully providing a calendar of activities for the months to come.

An action plan usually only takes an hour or two to pull together at the end of the planning process, but once done is something that you should try to keep constantly updated. I talk about creating your action plan in Chapter 12.

Deciding how far into the future you want to go

In this book, I focus on projections that cover the next 12 months (or the first 12 months from when a business starts trading). I do this largely for simplicity's sake. (The principle of creating a financial projection for 24 months is exactly the same principle as for 12 months — all you're doing is adding a few more columns.)

In practice, how far you should extend your plan into the future really depends on the nature of your business and how long it has been established. Here's what I suggest:

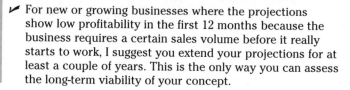

- ✔ For most new businesses, a 12-month financial projection works just fine. (Although most traditional business planning books talk about building financial projections for the next two, three or even five years ahead, I find that for new businesses, this long-term approach quickly spills into fiction territory. If you have no idea what sales you're going to make this month or next, how can you realistically predict what sales you'll make in three years' time?)

- ✔ For new or growing businesses where the projections show low profitability in the first 12 months because the business requires a certain sales volume before it really starts to work, I suggest you extend your projections for at least a couple of years. This is the only way you can assess the long-term viability of your concept.

✔ For an established business with three or more years of trading history, I recommend you extend your financial projections 24 months ahead.

Scoring Your Business

Are you still at the stage of thinking about your business idea and wondering if it's worth you even doing a plan? Maybe your business idea is still a glint in the eye, or maybe you've been mooching along half-heartedly with a new business for a little while now and don't know where you're headed. Just for a bit of fun (this is Chapter 1, after all), why not take a few minutes out and see how you and your business idea rate?

Use the scorecard in Table 1-1 if yours is a business that's been done before. By 'done before', I mean a business selling a service or product that others already provide, such as a gardening business, drycleaners or restaurant. Alternatively, if your business or business idea is a niche business or a new invention, use the scorecard in Table 1-2. For each question, a score of 1 is bad, and a score of 10 is good.

Wondering what a niche business is? A *niche business* is one that specialises in a small market segment. I came across a quirky example of a niche business just today. The company is called Dirty Rotten Flowers and creates unique bouquets for those who are wronged in love to send to the one who wronged them. (My favourite is probably the 'I Love You Not' bouquet, which includes a dozen twisted red carnations accompanied by a teddy bear embroidered with these very words.)

What score are you looking for? Overall, you probably want to get a score of 35 or more, although don't be dismayed if you score less. Chapters 2 to 5 provide lots of inspiration for developing your business ideas, Chapters 6 to 10 help you consolidate your financial skills, and Chapter 11 helps with the marketing side of things. You can return to this scorecard later in the planning process and see if your score improves.

Table 1-1	Rating a Business that's Been Done Before
Ask yourself this question and then score yourself from . . .	*1 to 10*
Can you think of something that will make your product or your service different from your competitors?	
Can you do something that will allow you to deliver a better product or service than your competitors?	
Are you going to be cheaper than your competitors?	
Do you love the day-to-day activity that this business demands?	
Do you know for sure that demand exists for your product or service?	
Do you (or someone in your team) have strong marketing skills?	
Are you well known locally, with a strong community network?	
Do you have enough start-up capital to give your business the best possible chance of success?	
Are you good with money, and able to understand budgets and stick to them?	
Is your vision for your business to build something that can ultimately run without your day-to-day attention?	
If you're in a relationship, does your spouse/partner support you in this venture?	

The very nature of business planning often means taking a slightly conservative approach, dealing with facts and figures rather than dreams and inspirations. But whatever you feel when working through your plan, stay tuned to that germ of inspiration that caused you to get to this point in the first place. Building any new business is a creative process and one that requires you to believe in yourself and your own abilities. This belief and creativity is what separates the natural entrepreneur from the nine-to-five office worker, and is ultimately the thing that will lead you to business success and its many associated rewards.

Table 1-2	Rating a Niche Business or New Invention
Ask yourself this question and then score yourself from ...	*1 to 10*
How unique is your product?	
If your idea is unique, do you have some way of safeguarding this idea from a competitor who might steal it?	
Do you know for sure that demand exists for your product or service?	
Do you have a clear strategy for launching your product or service?	
Can you do something that will allow you to deliver a better product or service than your competitors?	
Do you have enough start-up capital to give your business the best possible chance of success?	
Do you (or someone in your team) have strong marketing skills?	
Are you comfortable in the online environment (Facebook, Twitter, creating web pages and so on)?	
Is a window of opportunity emerging due to a change in the business environment, such as changing regulations, government grants or new technology?	
If you're in a relationship, does your spouse/partner support you in this venture?	

Chapter 2

Figuring Out What's So Special about You

In This Chapter

▶ Discovering the edge you have over others

▶ Scoring your strategic advantage from one to ten

▶ Writing your strategic advantage statement

▶ Revisiting your ideas on a regular basis

*E*ven if you have a business that's similar to thousands of others — maybe you mow lawns, own a hairdressing salon or tutor high-school students — you still need to come up with an idea that makes your business different from others in some way, or that provides you with a competitive edge.

Similarly, if your business caters for a very specific niche — maybe you sell gluten-free cookies or baby clothes made from organic cotton — you still need to identify how you can service this niche in a way that others can't, or what it is about your skills or circumstances that enables you to service this niche better than others.

If your business centres on an idea that nobody has tried before, you need to address why nobody else has bothered to try this idea until now and, in the event that you're successful, what prevents others from copying your idea straightaway.

The essence of what makes your business special, or more likely to succeed than others, is called your *competitive* or *strategic advantage*. I believe that this advantage is the single most important ingredient for ongoing business success — which is why, in this chapter, I focus exclusively on this very subject.

Understanding Strategic Advantage

In the introduction for this chapter, I mention the terms *competitive advantage* and *strategic advantage*. These two terms tend to overlap so much that I try to avoid getting bogged down in arguing about the distinction. I use the term strategic advantage in this chapter (because, after all, a true strategic advantage should ultimately result in a competitive advantage) but if you'd rather use the term competitive advantage in your business plan, that's just fine.

Looking at examples of strategic advantage

How can your business beat the competition, and what benefits can you provide that the competition can't? Here are some ways that your business may be able to secure a strategic advantage against others in the same industry:

- ✔ **Added value:** Can you offer added value in comparison to your competitors? Think 24-hour delivery, locally sourced product, a mobile service, or a quality of product or service that's beyond industry norms.

- ✔ **Exclusive distribution rights:** Do you have exclusive distribution rights to a sought-after product or service?

- ✔ **First cab off the rank:** Do you have a new idea that nobody else has tried before? Or a new way of doing something that makes the product or service better, quicker or cheaper?

- ✔ **Intellectual property:** Do you have unique intellectual property (IP) that customers want and that's hard to copy? IP includes copyright, patents and trademarks. If you're just getting started with your business, your IP could be as simple as a clever business name, an eye-catching logo or a well-chosen domain name (that is, a web address).

- ✔ **Location:** If you're a retailer, do you have a great location in a central shopping area? (Location is always *the* prime strategic advantage for retailers.) Or are you the only business providing a service in a particular suburb or region? Are the demographics of your location ideally matched to your business, or are you located in a central spot for freight and transport?

✔ **Lower costs:** Do you have an innovative way of doing things that reduces costs, creates economies of scale or significantly improves business processes?

✔ **Obsession and drive:** Do you have exceptional vision or drive? Is this drive connected with a particular obsession? (For example, think of Steve Jobs and his obsession about design.)

✔ **Perfectly matched team:** If you're in a business partnership of some kind, do you have a unique combination of skills and do you work well together as a team? (The synergy created by two or more people who have complementary skills and who work well together can be a force to be reckoned with, and something that's hard for competition to copy.)

✔ **Specialist skills:** Are you a specialist who has an insight into a particular industry that nobody else is likely to have? Maybe you can see a gap in the industry that nobody else is catering for, or maybe you can see a way to do something better.

Think of a business that you know that has been really successful (maybe a local business or a friend's business, or even a big name such as The Body Shop, McDonald's or Microsoft). Go through the list of different strategic advantages and think about which of these advantages could apply to these businesses.

Understanding how risk relates to gain

In most situations, the business with the highest potential strategic advantage is going to be the business that requires the most capital or involves the highest risk of failure. For example, imagine you had a really creative idea for a new smartphone app. Your idea potentially has great strategic advantage (a new invention or first cab off the rank), but is almost certainly quite risky. (Smartphone apps generally have high development costs, an unknown and untested market and may not even work that well when complete.)

In contrast, a safe business, such as lawn mowing, has few potential strategic advantages but involves the lowest risk of all. (The cost to set up this business could be as low as a few business cards.) Strategic advantages are hard to find for this kind of business because a lawn is only ever a lawn, and the owner will be limited in what to offer that others can't.

Thinking of potential strategic advantages for a business or service that lots of other people provide, and differentiating between your service and those of your competitors, is usually difficult. The upside of this kind of business is that the risks are usually lower; the downside is that it's always going to be tricky to charge premium rates or make above-average profits.

Justifying Why You Can Succeed

How can you apply the concept of strategic advantage to your business? Your first step is to identify what it is that makes you different, and apply a strategic advantage scorecard to your business concept.

If you're struggling to come up with anything that's special about your business — maybe you haven't stumbled on that winning idea quite yet — please do persist. The process of identifying your strategic advantage is even more important for you.

For a strategic advantage to be really worth something — in terms of the goodwill of your business or your likely financial success — the advantage has to be something that you can sustain over the long term.

I like to think that any really strong strategic advantage should have three attributes:

- ✔ **The advantage can't be easily copied by others.** The ideal strategic advantage is one that's really tricky for your competition to copy. Examples are a winning recipe or flavour (think Coca-Cola), a unique synergy of skills within your organisation, or expert knowledge that few others have.

- ✔ **The advantage is important to customers.** Think of the farmers who switched to growing organic produce in the early 1990s, before organics became more mainstream. Many of these farmers did really well because organics were so important to particular customers. (And although the advantage was relatively easy to copy, many authorities required a seven-year lead time with no chemicals before a farm could be officially certified.)

- ✔ **The advantage can be constantly improved.** If you can identify the thing that gives you an edge and constantly work this advantage, you have a strategic advantage that is potentially sustainable in the long term.

When Steve Jobs and Steve Wozniak started Apple, one key strategic advantage was that they were a perfectly matched team, and were passionate about design. The synergy of their skills was hard for others to copy, the beautiful design was something that customers really wanted and Apple was in a position to continually improve and develop this advantage.

Don't fall into the trap of thinking that being cheaper than everyone else is a clear strategic advantage. Being cheaper than everyone else usually means one of two things: Either your business isn't as profitable as it should be, or your competitors can grab your strategic advantage at any moment just by dropping their prices too. Usually, being cheaper than others is only a strategic advantage if you have some special skills, technology or volume of production that enables you to be cheaper.

Go to www.dummies.com/go/businessplanningessentials and download the Strategic Advantage Scorecard (also shown in Table 2-1). Rate your own business from 1 to 10 on each of the attributes shown on the scorecard (use 1 for no real advantage, and 10 for a winner strategic advantage that anyone else will find hard to beat). In the first column, apply a rating according to the benefits this advantage brings to your business; in the second column, apply a rating according to the benefits this advantage brings to your customers.

Table 2-1   Scoring Your Business's Strategic Advantage

Strategic Advantage	Benefit to Business	Benefit to Customer
Added value		
Exclusive distribution		
First cab off the rank		
Intellectual property		
Location		
Lower costs		
Obsession and drive		
Perfectly matched team		
Specialist skills		

You're probably wondering if a magic score exists that your business should achieve. It doesn't. But if you score 8 or more on any one count, this is a green light for you to concentrate on exploiting this advantage to the greatest extent possible. On the other hand, if you score below 3 on all counts, this indicates that unless you can come up with some new and creative ideas, your business is likely to yield similar (or even lower) returns than others working in the same industry.

Developing Your Strategic Advantage Statement

In this book, I'm pretty realistic about the written part of business plans. I know how few people actually write a 20- or 30-page business plan, despite their best intentions.

However, even if you do almost nothing else, I do recommend you formulate a statement of strategic advantage. In this statement, your purpose is to write down exactly what gives your business the edge over others.

Your strategic advantage statement is usually slightly different from your 'elevator speech' (something I talk about in Chapter 13) in that the statement may include information that you wouldn't necessarily share if 'giving the sell' about your business to a prospective customer.

Drafting your statement

Your strategic advantage statement needs only be a paragraph or two, but should include the following:

- ✓ Your company name
- ✓ How your product or service benefits your customers
- ✓ What makes your business different to your competitors, seen from the perspective of your customers
- ✓ Your strategic advantages (in other words, what knowledge, skills, synergy, team, technology or processes your business has that enables you to deliver these additional benefits to your customers)

I like to put this statement right at the beginning of any business plan because it's the knowledge of how you're different, and how you can succeed where others may fail or flounder, that needs to permeate every step of the business plan thereafter.

Figure 2-1 shows an example of an extract from a business plan for a handyman service, which has a focus on making homes toddler-proof.

Baby Busters provides a one-stop shop to help parents create a safe home. We not only assess the home for dangers, but also provide the required products and install them properly.

No other businesses within a 100-kilometre radius provide a similar service. We are different from competitors in that our installer (Dave) is not only a licensed carpenter, but also trained in occupational health and safety and has worked as a Risk Assessment Officer. Sandy has a marketing degree and currently works in real estate, which brings a special advantage in that she knows when people are moving into new homes and most likely to require this service.

Figure 2-1: An example statement of strategic advantage.

In Figure 2-1, Dave and his partner, Sandy, stress how the synergy of their skills and current occupations form their main strategic advantage. Some of these skills are also selling points for their business (for example, Dave's experience with risk assessment), but some are not (knowing when people are buying new homes so you can sell your product to them may be a strategic advantage, but it's definitely not a selling point).

Growing your advantages over time

Sometimes your strategic advantage isn't something that's blindingly clear from the moment you set out in business, but instead grows over time. Your skills grow as you develop in business, and your understanding of how you're different from the competition consolidates as well.

From time to time, you can review your strategic advantage by asking yourself these questions:

- ✔ What am I naturally good at? (Or what is my team good at?) Where do I feel I have been particularly successful in my business?

✔ What do I offer to my customers that's either cheaper than my competitors, better value or unique in some way?

✔ Does a point exist where what I'm naturally good at connects with what I do better than my competitors? If so, how can I build and develop this?

Looking Around for More Ideas

Keep an open mind for ways your business can be different or gain an advantage. Remember to review the match of your skills and what you're good at with the thing that your customers want that's going to make you different.

The internet is a great way to find new ideas and ways of doing business. If you're struggling to identify strategic advantages for your business, go online and look around the world at similar businesses to your own. What's their marketing strategy? Do they do anything differently with pricing? Opening hours? Added services? Is someone doing something that you could emulate?

Be prepared to revisit your ideas repeatedly and keep reshaping the concept that you have for your business until you can come up with a strong strategic advantage.

Chapter 3

Sizing Up the Competition

· ·

In This Chapter

▶ Getting motivated about understanding your competition

▶ Going undercover with Sherlock Holmes

▶ Choosing a strategy to set you apart

▶ Thinking about competitor and industry trends

· ·

I'm still surprised at how often I come across people planning to start a new business, or who are in the first couple of years of business, and are yet to research who their competitors are.

Detailed competitive analysis forms a vital part of any business plan and helps you establish what it is that your business is going to do better than others. As part of this analysis, you also need to think about future competitors — competitors who aren't yet a big deal, but could certainly become so if circumstances change.

In this chapter, I talk about doing a thorough competitor profile for key competitors, picking apart the differences between them and yourself.

I also go full circle and return to the questions any business person must ask themselves repeatedly: Given what competitors are doing and how they are faring, is your business model likely to fly like an eagle or sink like a stone? Or could you risk everything, and gain little in return?

Understanding Why Analysing Competitors is So Important

Your competition isn't just the marker of who you have to 'beat'. Your competition can be a source of inspiration or the benchmark that enables you to establish realistic expectations for your business. Your competition also provides a vital insight into where you can gain a possible edge.

Competitor analysis can also provide the reality check that prevents you from taking unnecessary risks. For example, in my local town a whole strip of cafes come and go with every change in season. If I were thinking about starting a cafe, a competitor analysis may quickly reveal that the rents in this strip are hideously high, the landlords are difficult and nobody is making enough profits to survive, let alone thrive.

On a more positive note, interacting with competitors can also point to potential opportunities. For many people, the seed of a winning business idea is sown by not being able to receive good enough service or quite the right product. So they think, *I can do better than that*, and a new business idea or marketing strategy is born.

Getting into the detail of competitor analysis can be just as insightful. If you're going to compete head-on with another business, you want to be right across the services that business provides and the prices it charges. Unless a massive undersupply exists, charging $20 more per hour is probably pointless if you're providing an identical service to someone who's working just next door.

Of course, price isn't the only thing that you're going to consider when comparing yourself against competitors. You also want to differentiate yourself from your competitors in ways other than price (always keep asking yourself what it is that makes *you* special) and you need to be able to convey this difference clearly in your marketing materials. Unless you know exactly what your competitors provide, you won't know how to sell your differences.

Last, and at the risk of sounding unscrupulous, researching how your competitors go about their business can often provide inspiration for stuff that you can do better. Pricing specials, weekend packages, discount offers, creative advertising or clever sales techniques are just some of the things you may decide to copy. After all, imitation is the greatest form of flattery (although your competitors may not see it that way!).

 When doing your competitor analysis, don't be hesitant to compare your business against big-time competitors such as supermarket chains or large franchises. While you may find it hard to imagine how your fledgling business could ever compete, the mass-market nature of these competitors often leaves niches that are underserviced, providing opportunities for smaller players.

Engaging in Cloak-and-Dagger Tactics

The time has come for you to don your dark sunglasses, felt hat and fake moustache. Adopt a foreign accent and pose as an undercover agent.

Doing a competitor profile

Making a list of possible competitors on the back of a beer coaster isn't enough. In order to truly understand your competitors, you need to do a full-on assessment of each one. (This detailed assessment probably won't end up being part of your final business plan, but does form the basis for your marketing strategies.)

Predicting exactly what you need to include in your competitor dossier depends on the type of industry you're in and also how practical it is to find out certain information. (Copying your competitors' bright ideas may be one thing, but hacking into their computer system is quite another.)

Your best source for all of this information is probably online (visiting your competitor's website or e-commerce store), but you may also be able to glean more information by checking out your competitors' stands if they go to trade shows, looking at competitor brochures, browsing through trade or business directories, chatting to suppliers or distributors, or talking to customers who have defected to your side of the fence. You may well have to go undercover and pose as a customer (or ask a family member to do so) — I know that such clandestine activity can feel a bit weird, but the results are usually worth it.

In Figure 3-1, I list a few questions you can use as your starting point for your competitor research.

The Competitor Analysis worksheet shown in Figure 3-1 is also available online at www.dummies.com/go/ businessplanningessentials.

Competitor Analysis

Competitor Name: _____ **Date:** _____

What customers does this competitor target in particular? ....

What are the hourly rates, or price per unit? ....

Do they offer any special pricing, discounts or pricing packages? ....

What image is this competitor trying to convey? ....

....

Do they have an area of specialty or a particular niche? ....

....

Do they offer any services that I don't? ....

....

Does this competitor seem to be doing well? ....

How long has this competitor been around? ....

How many employees do they have? ....

How savvy is this competitor in regards to technology? ....

Is this competitor active in social media? ....

What distribution networks does this competitor have? ....

....

....

What are the likely competitive advantages that this competitor has?....................

....

....

Figure 3-1: Building a dossier on each key competitor.

Mirror, mirror on the wall ...

Who's the fairest of them all?

One thing to remember when you compare yourself against others is that you don't need to be perfect, offer rock-bottom pricing or provide unbelievable service and availability. Instead, all you need to be is that little bit better than your competitor. For example, imagine an electrician starting a business in a new town deciding he wants to be the cheapest (always a risky business strategy, but nonetheless this can sometimes be an okay way to get started). He discovers that the next cheapest competitor is working for $45 an hour. In order to be competitive on price, this electrician doesn't need to sell his services for $35 an hour — $42.50 will do just fine and will meet the needs for those customers hunting around for the cheapest hourly rate.

Of course, price isn't the only variable that you need to consider, and Table 3-1 shows a detailed competitive analysis where this electrician compares himself with four other electricians in his local area, rating his competitors according to what they do better (or worse) than him.

Table 3-1   **Rating Head-to-Head Competitors**

Does this competitor ...	*Sparkies*	*Ed Power*	*PlugItIn*	*Wire & Co*
Have cheaper pricing than me?	Yes	No	No	No
Offer longer opening hours or availability?	No	No	Yes	Yes
Offer specific services that I don't?	No	Yes	No	Yes
Have better distribution or service a wider region?	No	No	No	Yes
Offer a larger variety of pricing packages?	No	No	Yes	Yes
Have more expertise and a higher level of skill?	No	No	No	Yes
Service all the niches that I service?	No	No	No	No

(continued)

Table 3-1 *(continued)*

Does this competitor ...	Sparkies	Ed Power	PlugItln	Wire & Co
Have respect and trust in the community?	Yes	No	No	Yes
Have an active social media presence?	No	No	Yes	Yes
Have a good online marketing strategy?	No	No	Yes	Yes
Have more capital and power to expand?	No	No	Yes	Yes

To do this competitive analysis for your own business, download the Current Competitor Analysis worksheet from www.dummies.com/go/businessplanningessentials. You may want to insert additional criteria against which to compare yourself, or cover more than four competitors in your analysis, but this template provides you with a starting point. The important thing is that you list your comparison criteria in the first column, and the names of the competitors that you're comparing yourself against in the first row. Below each competitor, write yes if they're better and no if you're better (or not applicable if this isn't relevant to you).

Choosing Your Competitive Strategy

Put simply, any business has three possible competitive strategies:

✔ To be the cheapest

✔ To be different from everyone else

✔ To serve a specific niche

In the next part of this chapter, I talk about choosing the competitive strategy that's going to work best for you.

Weighing up your options

After you complete the rating process for each competitor (refer to the preceding section), grab a highlighter pen (or use the Fill function in Excel) and highlight any rows that have 'no' in every column. For example, in Table 3-1, the electrician has 'no' against the question of whether his competition services all the niches he services. The fact that he's servicing a specific niche that others aren't servicing (in this case, a consultation service to make homes energy-efficient) highlights a clear opportunity. Pricing is also potentially an opportunity for this business, given that he is cheaper than three out of four of his competitors.

So what next? To put it simply, the electrician has three possible competitive strategies. He can try to lead on price, he can attempt to differentiate his services in some way or other, or he can focus on a specific niche.

In fact, any business, including yours, is faced with these three possible competitive strategies: cost leadership, differentiation or niche. You may choose only one of the strategies, you could choose two, or you may choose a combination of all three:

✔ **You can choose to be the cheapest (cost leadership strategy).** With this strategy, you're not necessarily the cheapest across all products you offer, or the cheapest for every service but, in general, you're aiming to compete on price. Price leadership can be a tempting strategy — after all, customers are always looking for a bargain — but is risky over the long term. Unless you have a strategic advantage that enables you to deliver your product or service more cheaply than your competitors, competing on price can mean weak profitability. (On the other hand, if you're just getting started, choosing to be cheapest can be a good strategy for gaining clients and building up experience.)

✔ **You can set out to create a point of difference (differentiation strategy).** If you have a business that's very similar to your competitors both in price and the service you provide, you can set out to differentiate yourself in some way. For example, an electrician could seek to make response time and punctuality a point of difference ('We'll arrive within 30 minutes of the agreed time or the first hour is free'), or could make availability a point of difference ('24-hour call-out service, 7 days a week').

Ideally, if you choose differentiation as your competitive strategy, you want to find a synergy between this differentiation and your strategic advantage (for more about strategic advantage, refer to Chapter 2). For example, maybe a strategic advantage for this electrician is that his wife also has a trade licence. Between them, they can offer a 24-hour service without worrying about leaving the kids unattended at home, and they can avoid the penalty rates that other businesses would normally have to pay if sending an employee out on a job in the middle of the night on a Sunday.

✔ **You can find a particular focus or niche (niche strategy).** With this strategy, your aim is to serve a specific market segment rather than dealing with the whole market. You can combine this niche strategy with a cost strategy, of course (by focusing on one specific niche, you may end up being the cheapest), and you can certainly combine a niche strategy with a differentiation strategy (because the differentiation itself becomes a niche). In *We Are All Weird*, written by Seth Godin and published by Brilliance Corporation, Godin argues that people are seeking choices more than ever, and that this competitive strategy is increasingly vital for any business.

You can choose cost leadership or differentiation as competitive strategies in their own right. However, if you choose a niche strategy, implicit in that is you're also choosing a differentiation strategy. (In other words, you can choose differentiation as your competitive strategy without having a niche, but by its very nature choosing a niche as your competitive strategy means that you're also choosing to differentiate.)

Matching competitive strategy to your strategic advantage

In Chapter 2, I talk about strategic advantage and explain that a true strategic advantage is something that your business has that offers real value to customers but that's hard for your competitors to copy.

If you managed to identify a strategic advantage, you may well find that this translates into a particular opportunity when you do your competitor comparison (as per Table 3-1, earlier in this chapter).

With these factors in mind, what you want to do is pick a competitive strategy (focusing on cost, differentiation or a particular niche) that complements both your strategic advantage and any opportunities you've identified in the competitive landscape.

Always try to pursue a clear strategy. If you choose to muddle along not doing anything that's clearly different to others, you will find it both difficult to compete and to establish a clear strategic advantage in the market.

Taking a Bird's-Eye View

One great reality check for any new business is to look at what's going on for your competitors and what the general trends in your industry are.

Have any of your competitors gone out of business in the last 12 months? How many? Conversely, have any new competitors come on the scene? How many?

With this in mind, what would you say is the general health of the industry in which you operate? Can you source any statistics (either from government or from industry bodies) regarding industry trends?

Thinking about future competitors

In the early planning stages of your business, it pays to spend some time thinking not just about who your competitors are right now, but also who your competitors could be in one, two or five years' from now.

Ask yourself questions relating to the following areas:

- ✔ **Automation potential:** Could any existing competitors automate their processes using advanced technology and, therefore, become more of a threat than they already are?

- ✔ **Big boys coming to town:** Could a franchise chain or large company move into your village, suburb or town and take lots of your customers? (In my village, the longstanding boutique wine store was decimated when two big liquor chains moved within 3 kilometres.)

- **Buyout of minor competitors by a larger competitor with more capital and muscle:** Could one of your existing competitors be bought out by someone with more capital and better distribution and, in the process, become a very formidable competitor? (Think about how some of the smaller gourmet food products have been purchased by supermarket chains and suddenly appear in every store.)

- **Offshoring of labour:** Could the services you provide be performed offshore instead? (Almost anything that's mostly labour and can be done on a computer is vulnerable to offshoring.)

- **Service offered online:** Could the service you provide be sold online and, therefore, open to international competition? (Even some things that I would never have imagined could go online have done so. I don't go to my local yoga class any more, but instead log onto a yoga website that offers hundreds of pre-recorded classes to fit any duration, level or style of yoga.)

Go to www.dummies.com/go/businessplanningessentials to download a Future Competitor worksheet, which lists each of the questions shown in the preceding list. Make notes against each of these headings, and think about what the future may have in store for your business.

Observing industry trends

To be strategic in business, you need an understanding of how the industry in which you're operating is faring, and what outside factors may affect this industry in the near future.

Here are the main areas I suggest you concentrate on:

- **Customer growth:** Is this industry experiencing growth in the number of customers?

- **Environment:** What environmental drivers affect your industry? (Consider climate change, ecological movements, environmental legislation, pollution and so on.)

- **Exchange rates:** How do exchange rate variations affect your industry? Is your business model dependent on a certain level of exchange rate?

> ✔ **Government legislation:** Could any government regulations, tax concessions, grant schemes or impending legislation affect your industry?
>
> ✔ **Technology:** What impact could technological change have on your industry? (Consider potential product obsolescence, changes in equipment, new customer demands, new skills and so on.)

If you like, you can download an Industry Analysis worksheet from www.dummies.com/go/businessplanningessentials. This worksheet has been populated with four examples. The easiest way to complete this worksheet is to add your own industry in the last column, looking at the examples to help along the way, and then delete these examples when you're done.

Responding to industry trends

The idea behind doing an industry analysis is to get a sense of what's happening overall in the industry. Of course, an industry that's in decline is going to be a whole load tougher (if not impossible) to succeed in than an industry that's growing very fast.

The traditional video rental store is an example I like to use when thinking of the risks of starting a new business in an industry that's in decline. I remember the video store that used to be in my village. The business was a solid one, and the store (as one of the only places open after 6pm) was always social and lively. Eventually it shut down and, in hindsight, I can look back and think the owners should have changed to renting more DVDs and fewer videos earlier; they could have downsized and halved the rent; they could have explored a niche market and developed an online presence. Pish tosh. For this particular business, there were probably not many options. My guess is the best thing the owners could have done (which for whatever reason they didn't) was close their business while they were still ahead.

If an industry is in severe decline, you want to be very wary of starting a new business in this industry. Chances are that change will be rapid and you will find it very hard to compete with established players who are willing to cut margins to the bone in order to survive.

Aside from an industry in decline, what about other scenarios —
such as enormous industry growth? Generally, industry growth
is a great thing for anyone involved, and if you're in the right
place at the right time, you can make handsome profits. The
flipside is that any industry experiencing rapid change carries
higher risks because the direction of change and new technology
can be hard to predict.

Part of the secret to mitigating this risk lies in matching the
internal strengths of your business against the potential
opportunities of the industry. And guess what? That's what the
next chapter is all about . . .

Chapter 4

Spotting Opportunities, Dodging Threats

In This Chapter
▶ Doing an honest no-holds-barred assessment of your abilities
▶ Spotting possible opportunities and threats
▶ Matching your strengths to opportunities and guarding against threats

A SWOT analysis (SWOT stands for Strengths, Weaknesses, Opportunities and Threats) is a keystone for any business plan.

The idea is that you make a frank analysis of what your business is good at and what it's not. Next, you think about all the possible opportunities for your business, such as new markets, new products or new ways of doing things. Last, you take a look at the threats facing your business, such as the state of the economy, industry trends or fearsome competitors.

With this process complete, you play the divine game of matchmaker, looking to see if there are any business opportunities that make a natural match for your strengths. Conversely, you look to see if there are any threats which present an unhappy synergy with your weaknesses.

A SWOT analysis done in this way provides an ideal starting point for strategic planning and is fundamental to business success. In this chapter, I explain how the whole deal works.

Looking at Your Strengths and Weaknesses

I'm sure you don't have to pause for very long to think of someone who always seems to choose the more difficult paths in life. Maybe you have a friend who's dyslexic but has chosen a career as a linguist, or you know someone in a wheelchair who travels the world.

Chasing one's dreams and persisting in the face of adversity is undoubtedly character-building and often deeply rewarding. However, in the world of business, it usually pays to be more strategic about where you channel your energies. What you want to do is identify the possible opportunities and see if you can match these opportunities against your natural skills and abilities.

Putting yourself through the griller

What are you naturally good at? Where do your weaknesses lie? Give yourself a performance rating on two counts against each key area in the following list. First, rate yourself according to how well you perform in that area. Second, apply a rating according to how important this attribute is for your business.

- ✔ **Computer systems:** How does your business rate in regards to reporting systems and sales management, and your ability to manage websites, custom software or any other IT requirements?

- ✔ **Customer service**: How does your business rate in regards to your ability to fulfill orders and respond to enquiries quickly? Do you communicate well with customers?

- ✔ **Finance:** How does your business rate in regards to keeping a good set of up-to-date books, invoicing customers and making sure you get paid on time? Do you have solid financial reporting, particularly regular Profit & Loss reports?

- ✔ **Management ability:** How does your business rate in regards to number of years' management experience, people-management skills, and your range of experience in different business situations?

✔ **People:** How does your business rate in regards to the balance and synergy of skills in the team, as well as the general vibe in the workplace?

✔ **Physical resources**: How does your business rate in regards to physical location and up-to-date tools and equipment?

✔ **Product or service:** How does your business rate in regards to the range of products on offer, as well as your technical expertise and ability?

✔ **Sales and marketing:** How does your business rate in regards to cold calling, direct sales or telesales? How are your negotiating skills, social media skills, and your ability to organise and run strong advertising campaigns? Can you write a good press release?

You can also print out a Business Performance quiz that corresponds to the questions above by going to www.dummies. com/go/businessplanningessentials.

When you assess your strengths and weaknesses, respond from the perspective of your business, rather than from you as an individual. Think of the collective skills that you, your employees, any family members, business mentors or outside consultants bring to the party. Also, keep your competition in mind when you rate your business on things such as customer service or marketing. (For example, you may be aware of small areas where you can improve your customer service but if you know that you beat all of your competition hands down, you can probably award yourself a rating of 'awesome'.)

When rating how important each function is for your business (sales, finance, people and so on), I suggest you always rate financial management as being important, regardless of what kind of business you own. Even if your business chugs along just fine and you're a shoebox-receipts kind of person, poor financial management is almost always a limiter to business success and growth.

Prioritising where you need to do better

If I'm a psychologist running a counselling business, chances are that cold calling or direct marketing skills aren't going to be that big a deal. On the other hand, if I'm selling a new product that few people have ever heard of, being able to sell anything to anyone is going to be an essential skill.

When rating your business according to how well it performs, take particular note of any areas where you rate yourself poorly in an area that you deem to be very important for your business. The combination of something being both important to your business but a weakness in your capabilities is an unhappy one.

Identifying Opportunities and Threats

In the SWOT analysis model, not only do you examine your internal strengths and weaknesses, but you also look at external opportunities and threats.

Opportunities and threats are generally things that can greatly affect your business but over which you have little control, such as changes in the economy or the arrival of new competitors on the scene. For you to stay one step ahead, the name of the game is to try to anticipate the impact these outside factors may have on your business.

For each of the following categories, ask yourself what opportunities and what threats lie in store. Remember that any change can be an opportunity or a threat (or even both) depending on where you stand in the scheme of things. Organise these opportunities and threats in two columns, similar to Table 4-1. (Keep in mind that Table 4-1 is a somewhat simplified example — your list will almost certainly contain a bit more detail.)

Consider the following:

- ✔ **Industry trends:** Is your business operating in an industry that's growing or in decline? What kind of changes are happening in your industry right now? (For more on this topic, look back to Chapter 3.)

- ✔ **New competition:** How likely is it that new competitors could affect your business? Do you have special skills or a strategic advantage that safeguards you from competition? (I talk more about strategic advantage in Chapter 2.) Or is the thing that makes your business so successful easy to copy? What if the competitor has more capital, a better location or superior marketing abilities?

✔ **Emerging technologies:** How is technological change going to affect your business? Could new technology end up putting you out of business? Or are you skilled in the direction that new technology is heading, which could be an opportunity?

✔ **Changes in demographics:** Demographic change is a long-term thing, but so (hopefully) is your business. If your business serves a local population (as opposed to having national distribution or being online), it pays to watch the trends in population patterns. (Running a children's toy store in a suburb with a rapidly growing retiree population and a declining birth rate may not be the most brilliant strategy ever.)

✔ **Changes in government regulations:** If your business is dependent in some way on government regulations (maybe you're a taxi driver, you work in health, or your business relies on government grants in some form or other), you're particularly vulnerable to changes in the political landscape. Ask yourself what impact changing regulations could have on your business and how you could respond.

✔ **Changes in the economy:** Is your business very dependent on the ebb and flow of the economy? Some businesses (for example, a business selling staple food products) are relatively stable regardless of what's happening in the economy; other businesses (such as those selling high-end luxury goods) tend to move in tandem with booms and busts.

✔ **Changes in your domestic affairs:** You won't find personal stuff listed in other business planning books, but if you're a small business, I know (from experience!) the impact that changes in your home life can have. A divorce can split business assets in two and turn a viable business into a struggling one, or the need for your family to move to another town for your spouse's job can dramatically affect your business. So if you think that a change of this nature is possible, don't be shy to include this in your plan.

Table 4-1	Summarising Opportunities and Threats
Opportunities	**Threats**

Analysis for iPhone app development company

Opportunities	Threats
Huge growth in demand	Growth in number of competitors
Opening up of labour market means possibility to hire overseas programmers at lower rates	Offshore labour market means new competition often at very low prices
Some clients willing to sign up for profit-share arrangements in lieu of lower charges	Changes in programming languages make it hard to keep up, especially with a small employee base and high cost of training
Lots of government contracts available as government bodies seek to create new apps for community info	Strong trend towards android phones, and expectation from clients for apps to be available for androids as well as smartphones

Analysis for solar panel installation company

Opportunities	Threats
Huge growth in demand	Some serious new competitors with major muscle
If proposed government changes go ahead, major subsidies for consumers	Exclusive distribution licence ends in two years
Schools and government bodies obliged by their own policy to stick with local suppliers	Rapid growth requires high borrowings and puts pressure on cashflow
	If new government, all subsidies could finish

When you're thinking about opportunities and threats for your business, you may also want to refer to the industry analysis process in Chapter 3. However, keep in mind that opportunities and threats in this context have a different scope than just one particular industry. For example, a global recession or a change in government isn't industry-specific. Or at the other end of the scale, the arrival of a new competitor may be a reflection of a growing population in one geographic region rather than an indication of general industry trends.

Some things can be either an opportunity or a threat, depending on your frame of mind. For example, maybe you perceive rapidly changing technology as a threat to your business. However, if you're willing to get creative, maybe you too can jump on the technology bandwagon and benefit from this change. Always stay open to new possibilities.

Pulling the Pieces Together

So far in this chapter you've looked at your personal capabilities (your strengths and weaknesses) and then examined the kind of opportunities and threats facing your business. Now you're ready to connect these different bits of information.

Putting theory into practice

The idea of a SWOT analysis is simple:

✓ Aim to build on your strengths but minimise your weaknesses

✓ Endeavour to seize opportunities and counteract threats

Are you ready to try your own SWOT analysis? Here goes:

1. **Make a list of the strengths and weaknesses of your business.**

   I explain how to do this earlier in this chapter in 'Putting yourself through the griller'.

2. **Make a list of possible opportunities and threats.**

   Refer to 'Identifying Opportunities and Threats' to find out how.

3. **Draw a grid similar to Figure 4-1.**

   You can use a whiteboard, butcher's paper or the nifty SWOT Analysis template that can be found at www. dummies.com/go/businessplanningessentials.

4. **Divide your strengths into two categories: Strengths that can help you take advantage of opportunities, and strengths that can help you deal with threats.**

5. **Write down these strengths in the first row of your SWOT grid, along with the related opportunities or threats.**

Strengths that help realise opportunities go in the top-left. Strengths that could help counteract threats go in the top-right.

6. **In the same manner, divide your weaknesses into two categories: weaknesses that may hinder you taking advantage of opportunities, and weaknesses that may make threats even more of a threat.**

7. **Write down these weaknesses, as well as the threats, in the second row of your SWOT grid.**

Weaknesses that hinder opportunities go in the bottom-left; weaknesses that exacerbate threats go in the bottom-right.

Business SWOT Analysis		
	OPPORTUNITIES	**THREATS**
STRENGTHS	*Write strengths that assist with opportunities here, along with a description of the opportunity*	*Write strengths that help counteract threats here, along with a description of the threat*
WEAKNESSES	*Write weaknesses that may hinder you from exploiting opportunities here, along with a description of the opportunity*	*Write weaknesses that may compound threats here, along with a description of the threat*

Figure 4-1: The principles of a SWOT analysis.

Translating your SWOT analysis into action

After you've completed your SWOT analysis (refer to preceding section), what next? Put simply, Figure 4-1 encapsulates four different business strategies:

- ✔ Aim to exploit any areas where your business is strong and is a good fit for an opportunity.

- ✔ Keep a watchful eye on any areas where your business is strong, but a threat may be looming.

✔ Try to improve on any areas where your business is weak but opportunities exist. (Maybe getting extra training, hiring employees with different skills or employing consultants.)

✔ Take pre-emptive action and attempt to get rid of any areas in which your business is weak but a threat is looming.

Imagine a company that's starting a new business developing iPhone apps. This company has identified that they have strengths in the area of marketing, but weaknesses in the areas of financial management and technical skills. They are also aware of the threats of cheaper labour from offshore employees, rapidly increasing competition, a general shift to the android market and likely downwards pressure in pricing.

Figure 4-2 shows how a SWOT grid may look for this company, matching strengths and weaknesses with opportunities and threats.

✔ **Top-left corner (where a strength meets an opportunity):** Strong marketing skills balance perfectly with strong growth in customer demand, just as the use of domestic employees (rather than offshore employees) make a good fit for growth in government contracts. The business should aim to exploit these strengths.

✔ **Top-right corner (where a strength meets a threat):** Strong marketing skills also serve to mitigate the threat of rapidly increasing competition. The business needs to keep a watchful eye on both marketing strategy and new competitors.

✔ **Bottom-left corner (where a weakness meets an opportunity):** A significant weakness is that the business only develops apps for the iPhone platform, and not for androids. The business should aim to improve this area of their business, particularly as the emerging android market is a clear opportunity.

✔ **Bottom-right corner (where a weakness meets a threat):** The weaknesses in financial management may create problems as downwards pressure in pricing is likely, given growth of overseas developers. This weakness and threat create an unhappy synergy, indicating an area in which the business needs to take action.

Example Business SWOT Analysis for iPhone App Company		
	OPPORTUNITIES	**THREATS**
STRENGTHS	*Strong sales and marketing skills, which are perfect for capitalising on huge growth in demand. Use of local (rather than overseas) labour means we're well placed to secure work from government organisations*	*Strong marketing skills will assist in meeting the challenges of many new competitors*
WEAKNESSES	*Programming skills in only one platform may limit potential, particularly if android phones continue to take market share from iPhones*	*Weaknesses in financial management may leave us exposed as cheap overseas labour puts downward pressure on pricing*

Figure 4-2: Plotting business strategy using a SWOT analysis.

Chapter 5

Separating Yourself from Your Business

· ·

In This Chapter

▶ Working out how far you want to take your business

▶ Playing with different roles to make a business work

▶ Creating a business that's independent from you

▶ Understanding that some businesses are harder to grow than others

· ·

*M*any years ago, I did some consulting work for a guy who'd started his own industrial welding business. The reporting systems for this business were a complete nightmare. As I trawled through the accounts, trying to make sense of it all, my client looked across the room at me and announced, in a somewhat apologetic tone, 'You know something? I'm a really good welder.'

For me, this brief interchange summarises the dilemma many business owners face. People start out in their business doing what they're good at, and what they love to do (whether this is welding, performing music or face-painting at kids' parties). But before long, they find they spend more and more time doing stuff they're not naturally good at, such as bookkeeping, looking through contracts, hiring employees or managing websites. Sometimes this extra work becomes such a burden that the joy of being in business is lost. Or sometimes the business owner rises to the challenge, thriving on these extra demands and enjoying the reprieve from day-to-day tasks.

In this chapter, I explore questions about what *you* want to achieve with your business. Do you plan to take on employees and grow your business? Do you have a unique concept that means you could potentially sell your business for a substantial profit in five or ten years' time? Or are you happy tinkering away in your home office, earning a modest income with little stress and few demands?

No answer is right, no answer is wrong. However, the process of creating a business plan provides an ideal opportunity for you to decide the direction in which you wish to head.

Deciding What Path You Want to Take

Generally, business planning books assume that you want to grow your business, take on employees, maybe even develop a franchise or expand internationally. (After all, the very expression 'business planning' implies an intention to expand and develop.)

However, in the first part of this chapter, I want to spend a bit of time exploring whether you feel this desire for expansion. Maybe you're quite content pursuing a small home-based part-time business or maybe you don't want the stress of taking on employees.

Taking a step back and thinking of all the self-employed people I know or have worked with, I can see that most people follow one of three different paths (or occasionally all three paths, but one after the other):

- ✔ A simple owner-operated business with no employees.

- ✔ A business where the owner focuses on providing the service but employs others to help run administrative functions of the business.

- ✔ A business built by the owner that then has a life of its own, where employees provide the services or manufacture products and the owner is in a management role. Ultimately, the owner may even seek to create a franchise.

The question you need to answer is which path do you want to take? Even though most business books imply that if you're serious about being in business the third path is the only way forward, this isn't necessarily true. Small owner-operated businesses may have less opportunity for profit, but profit is only one of the many motivators for being in business.

Doing the thing you love to do

A starting point for many small businesses is that a person goes into business to do the thing that they're experienced in, or possibly the thing that they've just completed studying. So the person who was working as a high-school teacher starts a business tutoring high-school students, the physiotherapist who was working at her local hospital opens her own practice, or the newly qualified chef opens a restaurant.

The upside of running a business this way is that you get to do what you love to do, and usually what you're good at. You also have the perks of self-employment (choosing your own hours, possibly charging more for your services and being your own boss).

The downside of being a solo owner-operator is often long hours, with no income when you're on holiday or if you're sick. The experience of being cleaner, shop assistant, bookkeeper, marketing manager and finance manager all within the course of a single day can be relentless, and you may end up feeling that you're a jack-of-all-trades but a master of none. Your business is utterly dependent on you; if you don't turn up, you don't get paid. In addition, the amount of money you can make from your business is always limited by the number of hours you're able to work.

Some people would argue that the kind of work involved with an owner-operator business, where it's just you and you do your own thing, defeats the purpose of going into business. They would argue that unless you want to conceive of a business that has a life of its own beyond yourself, you're better just to keep working for someone else. Otherwise, you're not really creating a business; rather, you're creating a job with a pile of overheads.

I disagree. Although I acknowledge that this small-scale kind of operation has its drawbacks, I've lived in a regional area and been self-employed for too long to be that naïve. Sometimes no jobs are available and the only option is to be self-employed. Sometimes you may have such substantial family commitments that your business becomes a relatively peripheral part of your life, and the income it generates is just a bonus, not the core. Sometimes the way you generate income is so personal, so idiosyncratic (maybe you're an artist, a faith healer or an inventor) that you can't conceive of a way that this business can be grown beyond yourself. All of these are perfectly valid reasons for being in business, yet staying small.

Even though you may have perfectly valid reasons for staying small, if you're currently self-employed and you have no employees — or you're planning to start a new business with this structure — do pause to consider what your options might be. Conceiving a way to run your business so that it can operate without you can be challenging, but is the only way forward if you want to generate profits that aren't directly dependent on the hours that you work.

Getting help and delegating what you can

If you're not content to be an owner-operator doing everything yourself, the first and most natural stage of expansion is usually to employ some assistance. Maybe you hire a bookkeeper, employ a casual labourer, or get assistance with marketing or website design.

Many experts and professionals end up with this kind of model. For example, our local orthodontist hires several employees (two receptionists, a dental hygienist and an office manager) but he is the only guy doing the actual orthodontic work — you know, the multi-colour braces and general teenage torture). Sure, he could probably hire another orthodontist to work for him, but he has a great deal invested in his reputation and, for whatever reason, feels he can't trust another person to provide the same quality of service.

In a way, the part of my business income that I generate writing books is similar. I employ a bookkeeper and office admin person, and occasionally get help researching topics, but at the end of day (and I confess that it's truly the end of the day as I write this), the only ones left standing are me and my cute little silver laptop.

This way of working is what many people choose. You get to do the thing you love and you can choose your own hours, be your own boss and usually make a decent living. And, unlike single owner-operators who do everything themselves, you can hire others to help with day-to-day business operations so that you can focus on doing the thing that you're good at.

The downside, of course, is that you're still 'it' as far as the business is concerned. You are your business, and your business is you. Your income is always limited by the number of hours you're able to work, and if you're on holiday or sick, the business doesn't generate income.

If your business has this kind of structure, you may find it hard to imagine how you can expand your business so that employees could provide the same services you currently do. However, nobody is indispensable, and no matter how smart or talented you are, chances are someone's out there who can do all the things you do.

 One of the tricks to making the leap to hiring others who can provide the services you currently provide is to imagine a little person sitting on your shoulder, watching everything you do and documenting your activities in a 'how-to manual'. This is the first step towards separating yourself from your business, so that you can describe to others the attitudes, skills and standards that you expect. (For more on this topic, see the section 'Documenting and building systems', later in this chapter.)

Building a business that's separate from you

The third path that you can take (refer to the preceding sections for an outline of the other two paths) is to create a business where employees are the ones providing your service or manufacturing your products. If you look around you, most medium-sized businesses fall into this category. For example:

- ✔ Our local plumbing company has a team of plumbers, each with their own van and apprentice, providing plumbing services. The owner occasionally helps out on tricky jobs, but mostly focuses on management and marketing.

- ✔ The place where my son learns piano is a music school, with lots of different tutors teaching different instruments. The owners teach sometimes, but other teachers run most of the classes.

- ✔ My neighbour runs a small chain of three cafes. He rarely cooks or serves tables any more, but focuses on the finances and management.

- ✔ A girlfriend of mine has a business selling baby sleeping bags. She still does the design and marketing, but she has moved production offshore and uses a distributor for sales.

Can you see that in each of these examples, the business owners have made a leap in how they think of their businesses? The plumber is now the manager of a plumbing services company; the music tutors started their own music school; the barista opened a chain of cafes; the seamstress runs a manufacturing company. In all of these examples, the owner no longer unblocks pipes, teaches violin, serves coffee or stitches fabric. In return, the potential for each of these businesses is that the owners can have more freedom and earn more money than they otherwise would have done.

For me, this transition from owner to entrepreneur is really exciting. Freedom from the shackles of the daily grind provides an opportunity to do the other things in life that were only dreams beforehand.

If you haven't made this transition, and your business is still dependent on you for pretty much every cent of income, my question to you is this: Have you ever consciously made the decision *not* to be entrepreneurial? Or, have you never really let yourself imagine how you could do things differently?

If not, do try to give the visionary in you some room to breathe. Spend time thinking about how you could grow your business and create something that has a life of its own.

In Chapter 10, I make a distinction between budgets and Profit & Loss Projection reports, explaining that a budget sets sales goals and spending limits that you must try to stick to, whereas a Profit & Loss Projection answers the 'what if' questions and enables you to model different scenarios. Even if you're just starting out in business, I suggest you spend some time experimenting with what your Profit & Loss Projection might look like in a few years' time, if you were to have a team of employees and possibly multiple locations or a much-increased product range.

Creating a way of doing business

The queen diva of all business models is, of course, the franchise. A *franchise* is where you figure out such a neat and unique way of doing business that this concept itself becomes something you can sell. A franchise embodies the whole way you do business, including buying policies, logos, marketing techniques, pricing, uniforms and more. Table 5-1 outlines various business models, and how specific owner-operator businesses could move into the franchise or international model.

Note: I'm not talking about purchasing a franchise here; rather, I'm talking about you building such a successful way of doing business that you create your own franchise.

Table 5-1	Moving from a Small Business to a Big Business	
Owner-Operator	*Business with Employees*	*Franchise/International Model*
Yoga teacher	Yoga school	Patented method of teaching and streaming online yoga classes
Plumber	Plumbing business with a team of ten employees	National plumbing franchise
eBay book sales	eBay business with three employees	eBay model for buying and selling books
A farmer selling homemade chilli sauce and pickles	A chilli sauce company with a recognised brand and national distribution	A method of manufacturing and distributing sauces/pickles that can be replicated worldwide
A corner cafe in the local town	A couple of cafes with several employees	A franchise restaurant chain
A fashion blogger selling clothes online	An online clothing store with 50 brands and national distribution	An innovative system (including software) for selling clothes online that can be replicated in other countries
Your business	....	....
	(fill in the blanks)	(fill in the blanks)

Creating your own franchise takes the requirement that you separate yourself from your business to a whole new level. For example, consider the plumbing company I refer to in the preceding section: When the owners (a husband-and-wife team) employed a team of plumbers to do the plumbing work, they entrusted others to provide the core service of the business on their behalf and, to do this, they had to provide a certain level of supervision and training. However, what if this plumbing company does really well and the owners decide to create a franchise? At this point, the owners need to analyse what it is that makes their business different. They need to quantify these differences and create systems so that others can copy these differences.

The upside of expanding to become a franchise is the opportunity to make very healthy profits. In many ways, a franchise is the ultimate realisation of the entrepreneur's dream.

Wearing Different Hats

Have you heard of a book called *The E-Myth* or *The E-Myth Revisited* (written by Michael Gerber and published by HarperBusiness)? This book has sold over 3 million copies, and the terminology that Gerber uses to describe the roles owners play in their businesses has become almost standard in some circles.

Gerber likes to describe the roles of a business owner as being technician, manager or entrepreneur. I may not describe these roles here exactly as Gerber might, but here's the general idea:

- ✔ **Technician:** These are people who work in their business, not on their business — the plumber who unblocks drains, the cafe owner who serves coffee or the freelance consultant who goes out to meet clients.

- ✔ **Manager:** A manager is someone who organises the day-to-day running of a business, ordering stock, looking at profit margins, paying the bills and replying to customers.

- ✔ **Entrepreneur:** An entrepreneur is the visionary, the person who's thinking of the business as a thing that's separate to the service it provides or the product it sells, and who is looking for ways to build the business and expand.

I really like this way of thinking of the roles in a business, because it goes a long way to explaining that feeling I've felt so often as a business owner — with all these balls in the air that I have to juggle. The idea is that if it's just you in your business (which it is for most people when they start out), you need to balance out these roles. The idea sounds simple, but is tricky to do.

These roles correspond to some degree with what I talk about earlier in this chapter. Someone who is happiest being a 'technician' often ends up not expanding their business, and instead typically provides services or makes products themselves (refer to 'Doing the thing you love to do' earlier in this chapter). A person whose 'manager' side wins out typically ends up organising others. This person is content to get employees to assist in running the business and is good at monitoring costs and ensuring efficient operations (refer to 'Getting help and delegating what you can'). The 'entrepreneur' personality is the one who's always looking for the winning idea, and is keenest to create a business with a life of its own (refer to 'Building a business that's separate from you' or 'Creating a way of doing business').

If your business is still pretty small, letting any one of the three roles of technician, manager or entrepreneur dominate at the expense of the others can be a problem. The technician will probably fail to grow the business, the manager may well fail to look to the future and plan for change, and the entrepreneur, if left to his or her own devices, may burn through a whole load of money very fast pursuing one idea after another.

What I think is so clever about the way Gerber identifies these roles is that you can apply this thinking to yourself and your own business. For example:

- ✔ Most people find that the technician role (doing the thing that they're good at, such as fixing pipes, teaching music or making a mean espresso coffee) feels comfortable and safe.

- ✔ The role of manager fits well with some people but not with others (many businesspeople hate having to think about money, tax, legals, schedules and so on, but others are relatively okay with this role).

- ✔ The role of entrepreneur is the role that comes hardest to most people. If you're inherently a bit conservative (as I confess to being myself), what happens is whenever the entrepreneur voice pipes up with a good idea, the conservative manager voice calls out 'Oh no, that's way too scary'. The entrepreneur and manager are so busy tussling away that the only person left to do anything is the technician, who continues to get on with the job. And then nothing changes.

The way to move on from this situation, and give all three roles a part to play, is to build a business that stands on its own feet. I outline the key steps to building a business in the sections that follow.

Building a Business with a Life of its Own

Creating a business with a life of its own is generally the best way to gain more freedom and flexibility, and hopefully more profit to boot. However, the transition to creating a business with its own identity, separate from you, isn't always easy, so here I provide some guidelines on how you may be able to make this happen.

Defining your difference

The first step in giving your business some life force of its own is to be clear about what it is that makes you different. I spend a heap of time deliberating on this very topic in Chapter 2, so I won't repeat myself here. Suffice to say that you must identify what makes your business different, and this difference must relate to the identity of your business, and not you personally.

Some examples may help to set this in context:

- ✔ A drycleaning company uses alternative chemical processing, arguably better for the environment and for those with sensitive skin.

- ✔ An online clothes store offers multiple views of each item of clothing, and provides recommendations as to the body types each garment is best suited for.

- ✔ A mechanic workshop offers a free home drop-off and pick-up service, and routinely details all vehicles as part of any service or repair work.

None of the preceding ideas are particularly revolutionary but, if executed well and combined with a cohesive marketing strategy and company commitment, they have the potential to make these businesses stand apart from others.

I find that business owners can be very vague regarding what it is that makes their business successful, especially smaller businesses, where the owner is still very much hands-on. To use the mechanic workshop example from the preceding list, this mechanic may offer free home drop-offs and detailing, but is this really the reason for the workshop's success? Or is it that the head mechanic is such a lovely guy that customers instantly warm to him? Or perhaps the workshop is the only repair service within a 10-kilometre radius?

Without an understanding of what makes this business successful, the owner is vulnerable. If the drawcard is the gorgeous mechanic, what might happen to the business if he leaves? If the lack of competition in a 10-kilometre radius is the reason for steady business, what might happen if another mechanic opens up shop nearby?

You can try to deduce the reasons for your success using a few techniques:

✔ If your business operates in more than one location, experiment by trialling specific services or marketing techniques in one location but not the other, and see what happens.

✔ Return to the competitive analysis you did in Chapter 3 (or if you haven't already done it, do it now). This objective comparative process is a good way to get a sense of why your customers come to you.

✔ Ask your customers why they love you! (And if they say it's because of your good-looking head mechanic, sigh long and loud.) You can ask customers face to face, run surveys, put up quick questions on Facebook, or do whatever fits your customer base best.

✔ Try opening a new location and replicating your success in the first location. If the new location performs differently, try to get to the bottom of why.

✔ If you think that part of your success is due to something relatively simple (I think of my local butcher who, after each interaction, looks at me with a smile and says 'Can I get you anything else today?' — even if a queue of people is waiting behind me), then try measuring sales when you employ this technique or strategy for a week, and compare sales to another week when you don't do this.

If you can figure out why you're successful, and measure how much difference this strategy, product or technique makes to your business, you're well on the way to being able to replicate your success and grow your business.

Documenting and building systems

One of the things that a franchise offers, in contrast to other businesses of a similar type, is consistency. As my husband likes to say in a satisfied voice regarding the coffee he buys from a certain fast-food chain, 'This bunch make the best worst coffee in the world'. In other words, he knows the coffee is going to be average, he knows it won't be that hot, but still it hits the spot and it's the same every time, wherever we are in the country.

This consistency is one of the secrets to expanding a business beyond one location, building a brand or even preparing your business to become a franchise in its own right. Take the example of my aunt who ran a guesthouse in the wilds of northern Scotland for 30 years or more. She was a wonderful hostess, but occasionally she'd be away for the weekend or even for a week or two. How could she guarantee that her guests would get exactly the same quality of experience when she was away as when she was there?

A happy customer may share the love with one or two people, but unhappy customers share their disgruntlement with ten. If you can get rid of the hit-and-miss element that plagues so many businesses, positive word-of-mouth recommendations may be almost all the marketing you need.

So how do you guarantee consistency, particularly as your business grows and you're not around to serve each customer or supervise each employee? The answer is in procedures and documentation. First, you figure out what it is that your business does well (which I refer to in the preceding section); next, you articulate this difference in words in a way that employees can follow.

Here are some examples of how to provide a consistent experience for customers and build a distinctive brand:

> ✔ **Checklists:** For any complex activities, where employees need to fulfil several tasks in a specific sequence, create a checklist. For example, if customer orders are quite complex in your business (maybe you need to check

quantities, availability, delivery dates, payment methods and more), a checklist ensures nothing gets forgotten.

✔ **Complaints procedures:** Do you know that one of the ways to make customers happiest is to do everything you can to fix something when they complain? However, the gentle art of responding well to a grumpy customer isn't something that comes naturally to most people, and so procedures for dealing with complaints are essential.

✔ **Customer service procedures:** Ideally, you need a procedure for any customer interaction that happens on a regular basis, whether for a customer enquiry, order or sale.

✔ **Manufacturing procedures:** If you're a manufacturer, even if you're operating on a relatively small scale, making things to sell locally or at markets, the quality of your product needs to be the same each time. Sounds simple, but imagine you're making homemade jams, and the quality of produce available varies according to the time of year. In this scenario, you may need to limit production to certain times of year in order to guarantee consistency.

Similarly, if you've been manufacturing products yourself and you're now ready to delegate this process, you need to document exactly what you do, using precise quantities, times, production methods and so on.

✔ **Phone scripts and email templates:** I can feel you wincing a little here, as you wonder if you're really so dictatorial that you can bear writing out scripts for employees to follow when they answer the phone, or templates for when they reply to emails. Remember two things, however: Firstly, what you're trying to achieve is consistency for the customer; secondly, if you have spent time figuring out the ingredients that have made your business successful and you know that how you answer the phone or reply to emails is part of this success, then, of course, you want to be able to repeat this formula, time and time again.

✔ **Presentation:** As someone who hates uniforms in almost any shape or form, I squirm a little as I write this. But businesses love uniforms for the reason that they provide consistency for the customer and reinforce the company's image. Even something as simple as a polo shirt with your company logo monogrammed on the front can make a difference to how customers perceive you.

✔ **Rates and pricing:** Standardised rates and pricing are a must. So if you tend to quote on a somewhat intuitive basis for jobs, you need to spend time figuring out a method for pricing and stick to that instead.

If you're still small and you're thinking about how to expand your business, one great source of inspiration (if available) is to look at franchises that offer a similar service or product to your own. For example, if you're starting a lawn mowing business, take a look at how the lawn mowing franchises approach their branding, marketing and customer service. If you're starting a bookkeeping business, look at the bookkeeping franchises and how they organise their pricing and services. I'm not suggesting you steal intellectual property here or that you try to copy the systems of a franchise without paying to belong, rather that you take a look at the franchise's general approach and use this as inspiration. (Or, of course, you may even consider becoming a franchisee.)

Setting goals for you and your business

I've worked as a business consultant for more than ten years now, and I've noticed a certain quality in the handful of very successful businesspeople I've encountered during this time. Each of these people have had a very specific goal in mind, and they've been possessed by an inner drive to meet this goal.

Interestingly enough, these goals have been ultimately personal, rather than business-orientated, such as the desire to be able to retire by the age of 50 on a guaranteed income for life, or the dream to be able to buy a house for each one of the children, or to be able to work only 20 hours a week and still be financially secure.

If you're trying to create a business that grows and is ultimately independent of you, ask yourself what you want to achieve from this growth. Do you have a specific financial goal or a certain time frame? If not, spend some time thinking what this goal might be, and then building your business plan around this goal.

Timothy Ferriss (author of *The 4-Hour Workweek*, published by Crown) has interesting perspectives on long-term goal setting. One of his appealing arguments is that someone who works 8 hours a week and earns $50,000 a year is actually much richer than someone who works 60 hours a week and earns

$200,000 a year. He argues that income is relative, and profit not the only performance measure.

While setting goals is an important part of business success, just wanting to be a millionaire isn't enough. You need to ensure that your business has some kind of competitive edge or winning strategy (refer to Chapters 2 and 3 for more on this topic) and you need to understand how to build on this strategy with good systems. Unless you have these elements in place, ambitious plans to open a new shop every six months or become an internationally recognised brand are just pie-in-the-sky.

Planning for a graceful exit

One of the best ways to get yourself into the mindset of thinking of your business as independent from you is to imagine selling it.

Always try to have an exit plan simmering away, even if you don't plan to sell any time in the immediate future. Ask yourself the following questions: If I were to sell this business today, what could I get for it? Can this business run independently of me? What assets or business systems do I have to sell? How can I maximise the price I can get for this business?

Appreciating the Limitations of Your Business

When thinking about how to build a business with a life of its own, keep in mind that some businesses are much harder than others to expand. Here are some of the kinds of businesses that can be hard to grow, along with why:

- **Businesses limited by physical constraints or high start-up costs that require substantial capital:** Farmers are an obvious example here, limited by the amount of land they have and lacking capital to expand. Other examples could be a professional truck driver limited by the high capital cost of additional trucks, or the capacity of a guesthouse owner to expand due to the high cost of purchasing real estate.

- **Businesses based on the artistic skills of the owner:** Examples include a classical pianist performing around the country, a stand-up comedian or a theatre producer. Sure, you could team up with other artists in a similar field, but the actual core of what you do (such as playing virtuosic piano) is almost impossible to delegate.

✔ **Businesses making products that require very specific skills, particularly those of an artistic nature:** For example, glass blowing, fine-art painting and pottery. Custom manufacturing of one-off goods also falls into this category, where the craftsperson (such as a cabinet-maker) builds a reputation that is very much linked to that person as an individual, rather than to the business.

✔ **Businesses with expert services where the service provided is very much associated with the individual providing the service:** Think specialist medical professionals (acupuncturist, paediatrician, orthodontist) or specialist consultants (business mentors, human resources consultants).

✔ **Businesses servicing a rural location where the owner provides the services and expansion involves too much travel:** Our local horse dentist (yes, there is such a thing as a horse dentist!) springs to mind.

The more entrepreneurial personalities may be reading the preceding list thinking that I'm lacking imagination, and that the businesses in the list could be expanded in plenty of ways. The artist could commercialise her images as cushions, postcards or wallpaper; the horse dentist could set up an online consultancy; the cabinet-maker could spend oodles on high-end marketing and build up an international reputation. In my defence, I'm not saying that these businesses are impossible to grow — I'm just saying they're harder to grow than others. (And besides, the artist may not want to design wallpaper and online horse dentistry may prove massively impractical.)

If your business falls into one of the categories outlined in the preceding list and you're having problems imagining how you separate yourself from your business, hop onto the internet and search worldwide for the product you sell or the service you provide. Look for examples of others similar to you and how they have grown their business to be something bigger.

Although businesses with expert services can be hard to expand, for those who manage to do so and build a network of professionals who provide a high consistency of service, the rewards can be substantial.

Chapter 6

Budgeting for Start-Up Expenses

. . . .

In This Chapter

▶ Making a list of everything you need and how much it's likely to cost

▶ Differentiating between expenses and how to account for each one

▶ Considering how much finance your business needs to get off
   the ground

▶ Selling your soul to the devil, taking out loans and more

. . . .

*I*f you're planning to start a new business or expand your
existing business in some way, chances are you're going to
need a bit of cash behind you. The question is, of course, how
much?

When starting a business, your budget must allow for not only
new equipment, vehicles, stock and other big-ticket items,
but also the variety of additional expenses you're bound to
encounter in the first few months of trading. You may also
need additional finance for living expenses until your business
becomes profitable.

In this chapter, I talk about pulling together your start-up budget
and working out different types of expenses so that you can
plan how much cash you're going to need. I also talk about
navigating the dark perils of finance, including the pros and cons
of business loans, credit cards, equity partners, leases and last
(but not least) borrowing funds from your benevolent and long-
suffering family.

Creating a Start-Up Budget

Creating a budget for start-up expenses is a good idea, no matter how large or small your proposed business. Unless you know how much capital you're going to need to get started, you won't have any idea about how much finance is required, nor will you have a sense of the risk involved.

If you're still at the conception stage for your business — maybe you're testing your product at local markets or trialling the service that you offer — you're probably still working from home or manufacturing on a small scale. As part of the planning process and testing the long-term viability of your business idea, I suggest you create a start-up budget for how much money you would require if you were to manufacture your product on a large scale or if you were to set up a proper office servicing a wide range of clients.

Purchasing materials and inventory

If you're a manufacturer, retailer or wholesaler, your start-up budget must include the initial purchase of products for resale. In order to create this budget, you need the following information:

- ✔ **If you are a retailer:** Your start-up budget must include an estimate of the cost value of stock (including freight) you will need to have on your shelves on the first day that you open.

    Most retailers, other than those selling fresh produce, have at least two months' worth of stock at any one time. If you're importing goods from overseas, you will almost certainly require more than two months' worth of stock (either in your shop, or already in transit).

- ✔ **Manufacturers:** The initial stock that you require entirely depends on whether you're doing custom manufacturing (in which case you probably only need to invest in display goods) or whether you're doing bulk production (in which case you may need a minimum initial volume in order to keep your costs down).

- ✔ **Distributors/wholesalers:** The value of stock required depends on the lead time from your suppliers. If your suppliers can deliver to you overnight or within a couple of days, you'll need to hold much less stock than if you're importing goods from overseas.

From a bookkeeping perspective, when you buy goods that you plan to resell, or when you buy materials that you plan to manufacture into a finished product, these purchases aren't cost of goods sold, nor are they expenses. Instead, bookkeepers allocate stock purchases to asset accounts called Inventory, Stock on Hand or Raw Materials. This distinction between an asset and an expense is crucial to understand when you're assembling your financial projections. If you show all the stock or raw materials required for starting your business as an expense, your projected Profit & Loss could look very miserable indeed. (For more about the difference between cost of goods sold and expenses, see Chapter 8.)

Listing your start-up expenses

In Table 6-1 I show a possible format for listing start-up expenses. I suggest you create this list using spreadsheet software such as Excel (this way, if your forecasted figures change, all the totals recalculate automatically).

Go to www.dummies.com/go/businessplanningessentials to access the budget shown in Table 6-1 as an Excel spreadsheet. Print out this document or open the spreadsheet on your computer and place a dollar estimate against each line.

Making your start-up expense estimates is pretty straightforward, but here are some pointers to help along the way:

- ✔ If an expense isn't relevant, just enter $0.00 as the value, or delete this row entirely.

- ✔ If something is missing from this list, just add another row. Remember, however, that you're budgeting for start-up expenses, not ongoing expenses. (If you're not sure what counts as a start-up expense, skip ahead to the section 'Separating Start-Up Expenses from Operating Expenses', later in this chapter.)

- ✔ Have you already purchased some business assets using your own funds? See the section 'Including expenses paid for out of personal funds' later in this chapter for more details regarding whether to include these assets in your start-up expenses.

- ✔ If consumer tax applies in the country or state in which you're operating (for example, sales tax in the United States, VAT in Canada or the United Kingdom, or GST in

Australia and New Zealand) and you know that you'll be able to claim a refund for any tax you pay, show your start-up expenses excluding, rather than including, tax.

Table 6-1	Start-Up Expenses Budget
New Equipment or Tools	*$*
Computer systems, including POS equipment	
Vehicles, including special fit-out, if required	
Office furnishings, tools or equipment	
Premises Fit-out	
Council fees, if necessary	
Fit-out of new premises	
Lease agreement fees	
Rental bond and rent in advance	
Other Start-up Expenses	
Accounting and consultant fees	
Insurance (public liability/business indemnity/property insurance)	
Internet and telephone connection, plus network cabling	
Legal fees and registration of business name	
Licence fees	
Marketing materials and brochures, including signage	
Security bonds for electricity, gas and phone	
Stock for resale	
Training of staff	
Website design and construction	
Other (describe here)	
TOTAL	*$___.__*

I often get asked how much is reasonable for a start-up budget. My answer is that I've seen business start-ups that require not one brass razoo, and others that require several million dollars. If you're not sure about the accuracy (or completeness) of your start-up budget, I suggest you bounce the figures off your accountant or business adviser.

One thing I have noticed is that people planning a new retail business often seem to underestimate start-up expenses. Items such as shop fit-out and opening stock for resale are invariably more expensive than expected. Make sure you're budgeting enough to cover all likely expenses.

Including expenses paid for out of personal funds

Have you already purchased an asset in your own name that you're intending to use for business purposes (likely examples are a computer or vehicle)? If so, should you show this item in your budget for start-up expenses? The answer depends, as follows:

- ✔ If you're setting up as a sole trader or a partnership, your start-up budget doesn't need to include assets that you've already purchased.

- ✔ If your business is going to have a company structure and you require the company to reimburse you straightaway for this asset, then yes, include this asset in your start-up budget.

- ✔ If your business is going to have a company structure but you're happy for the company to make use of an asset that you own while it's getting established, you don't need to include this asset in your start-up budget.

Adding enough to live on

Most businesses don't make any profit in the first six months and, in fact, many businesses make a loss during this time. For some businesses, the period before you see any profits may be even longer.

When budgeting for a new business, you not only need to budget for business expenses, but also your own living expenses. Quite how you do this depends on your circumstances, and whether you're continuing to work another job while your business gets established. Chapters 7 through to 10 explore operating budgets in detail, pulling together the different elements of your financial plan. When you complete this process, you should be able to ascertain whether you require any additional finance for living expenses.

 While your budget for start-up expenses is an essential first step, this budget doesn't necessarily provide a clear indication of how much you need to borrow — you only know that for sure when you complete the rest of your business and personal budgets. See Chapters 7 to 10 for more on this.

Separating Start-Up Expenses from Operating Expenses

If you're new to business, you may find it hard to differentiate between start-up expenses and operating expenses. This difference is crucial in order for you to calculate how much start-up finance you require and to report accurately on business profitability. For example, if you spend $500 painting the inside of your new office, does this count as a business start-up expense, or is it just repairs and maintenance?

The answer — in terms of your business plan and financial reporting, but not necessarily your tax return — is that if something is a one-off expense that's related to getting your business started and you don't expect to have this expense again as part of day-to-day trading (or not for a little while at least), you should treat this as a start-up expense.

For example, if you rent a new office or shop and you spend money on fitting out the premises, building shelves, adding carpet or painting, these are good examples of start-up expenses. (However, if you repaint or re-carpet the office in a few years' time, the expenditure would count as repairs and maintenance.)

Other items such as logo design, business stationery, marketing materials or packaging design are also good examples of start-up expenses. Sure, you'll almost certainly spend money on more marketing materials in the future, but you're unlikely to have such a big expense all in one go.

What you're trying to do is distinguish between all those initial expenses that come in a rush when you start your business, and separate these from the ongoing expenses. This is the only way you can establish how profitable your business really is in those first financially delicate months of trading.

A *start-up expense* is a one-off expense related to starting your business or purchasing an asset that your business requires. An *operating expense* is an ongoing expense that will feature as a regular part of running your business.

Assessing How Much You Really Need

If you've been reading through this chapter from the beginning, hopefully you have an idea of how much money you'll require to get your business started. You'll know how much you need for equipment, vehicles, office or shop fit-out, as well as how much you need (if anything) for opening stock. In addition, you've started thinking about whether you'll need additional funds to see you through the first few months of business while you get yourself established.

In other words, although you won't have a final figure for how much you may need in the way of finance, you should have a rough idea. At this point, you can start thinking about three things:

- ✔ If you don't have the necessary savings, will you be able to borrow the money?

- ✔ How much finance will you need, and what will the likely repayments be?

- ✔ Will repayments be affordable in the first year or two of your business — or will this level of borrowing bring an unacceptable level of risk and/or stress?

Depending on the answers to these questions, you may want to review your start-up budget. Although earlier in this chapter I stress the importance of giving your business every possible chance of success by budgeting enough (refer to the section 'Listing your start-up expenses'), you may find that you can pull back or delay on some spending without the business suffering unduly.

Here are some tips for pruning your start-up budget:

- ✔ **Consider leasing rather than buying assets outright.**
  Finance that's secured against an asset such as a vehicle is
  usually pretty easy to obtain, and preserves your cash so
  that it can be used as working capital instead.

- ✔ **Be realistic.** You may really want that brand new speed-
  machine, but unless your vehicle is an essential part of the
  brand and image of your business, you can almost certainly
  do without.

- ✔ **Consider buying stuff second-hand.** Again, second-hand
  stuff isn't as glamorous as new and shiny stuff, but may do
  the job just as well.

- ✔ **Look at renting equipment.** If your budget includes
  new equipment, consider whether you could rent this
  equipment on an occasional basis while your business
  builds up.

Always guard your *working capital* (that is, the difference
between your current assets and current liabilities) as a tigress
guards her cubs. Even if you think you have enough cash to
purchase everything your business needs to get started, if your
business is successful and grows at any kind of pace at all, the
growth itself is likely to gobble up your ready cash.

Understanding Finance Options

After deciding how much finance (if any) you require (refer to
preceding sections), the next task is to find a willing victim to
cough up the cash. A bank is usually the most obvious option,
but other sources of funds include finance companies, equity
partners, and family or friends.

At this point, spend some time confirming exactly how much
you'll be able to borrow. If you have no steady income and no
collateral (that is, assets such as your home against which the
bank secures its loan), you may find that the bank refuses to
lend you anything. This may mean you need to rethink your
business plan or delay the start date while you save additional
funds.

Getting into bed with the bank

Before you jump into a long-term relationship with any lender, be clear what you're getting into. Here's a quick summary of the kinds of finance available:

- ✔ A *business loan* usually works like an ordinary home loan — you borrow a fixed amount and commit to regular repayments over a certain number of years. A business loan is well suited for start-up finance, debt refinancing or financing business growth.

  With business loans, the upside of structured repayments is that you're likely to pay off the loan relatively quickly. The downside is the bank usually offers a relatively short term on business loans (five years is quite standard) meaning that repayments are high even in the early years when the business can least afford it.

- ✔ A *business lease* can work in different ways depending on how you structure the lease. This kind of finance is almost always secured against a specific item of equipment or vehicle. Essentially, the finance company buys the asset on your behalf and then you make regular monthly payments for an agreed amount of time. Depending on the lease agreement, you will either own the asset outright at the end of the loan term, or you will be able to purchase it for a reduced price.

  Leases are relatively easy to obtain for existing businesses (because they're secured against the asset itself) and help preserve your valuable working capital for things that are harder to obtain finance for (such as an increase in inventory or financing of accounts receivable).

- ✔ A *credit card* is the easiest type of finance to obtain, but is usually limited in how much you can borrow. Credit cards also involve the highest rate of interest. Generally, credit cards are best for short-term borrowing of relatively small amounts, and are a poor choice for start-up business finance.

- ✔ A *line of credit* works a little like a regular bank account, except the balance is in the red, not the black. You can use the loan for all your business banking, including both deposits and withdrawals. You have a credit limit on the account, and it's your choice whether you pay off the principal or pay interest only. Lines of credit are ideal for on-demand working capital and improved cashflow.

Although a line of credit offers great flexibility for your business, you do need to have a disciplined nature to force yourself to pay off the debt. (If you never reduce the principal outstanding on your line of credit, you end up paying more interest than on a regular business loan.)

Offering up collateral

Almost all banks require some security against borrowings and, unless you're still renting, the most obvious security is usually your own home. While you probably feel reluctant to offer your home as security, you may find that you don't have much choice in the matter, or that a business loan secured against your home attracts substantially less interest than a business loan that's unsecured.

Even if a business loan is in your name only, if you guarantee this loan against a property that's jointly owned, it's extremely likely that both parties (that is, both you and your best beloved) are jointly liable. This means that if the relationship breaks down, you get sick or even if you die, the other person may be legally obliged to repay the debt. For this reason, involving your better half in the decision about using the family home to secure a business loan is vital.

Seeking equity partners

In the preceding sections I talk only about *debt finance*, meaning that to get cash for your business, you go into debt. However, the other major source of business finance is *equity finance*. With equity finance, you receive funding from an investor in exchange for a portion of ownership of your business.

The idea with most equity finance is that investors — sometimes referred to as *business angels* — buy into your company, offering funds and expertise in return for part-ownership. The investors don't receive interest on these funds, but instead are looking for a return through long-term capital gain. Because the investors are exposed to the risk of your company failing, they usually look for businesses with a strong history of growth and higher-than-average returns.

The advantages of equity finance include the ability to raise funds even if you don't have security or collateral to offer, meaning that your financial structure is more stable. In addition, your business can hopefully benefit from the investor's management expertise. On the downside, an outside investor means that you no longer have complete control of your business. You may find it hard not being able to make decisions without consulting others first, especially if you're used to running your own show, and conflict between you and the investor becomes a real possibility.

Borrowing from family

Borrowing from family can be both the easiest and the hardest way to secure finance, all at the same time.

When writing this chapter, I drafted these last couple of paragraphs about borrowing from family and friends and then decided 'Nah, I'll just delete this stuff — it's all so obvious.' And so I did. The very next day, I bumped into the sister of an old client of mine and we got chatting. The father of my client had lent my client a large sum of money many years ago, and my client had repaid his father assiduously in the intervening period until the debt was completely cleared. As far as I was concerned, this particular scenario was a happy one, where none of the stuff that so often goes awry with family loans had occurred. Little did I know, the sister of my client, many years after this loan had been offered and then repaid, was still upset. It turned out that she had approached her father for finance as well, but her father had said he couldn't, because he had no money left to lend. The sister had missed out on the purchase of the farm she wanted, and had nursed a resentment against her brother for years.

You will find many ways to make money in your lifetime but you will only have one family, and your family relationships are probably more valuable than anything else in your life. If you're considering borrowing from your family, pause first to think how other siblings may feel and what would happen if you fail to repay these funds. If your siblings could feel resentful or your family would suffer in any way if you were to fail to repay these funds (and failure in business, no matter how optimistic you currently feel, is always possible), then think again. You may be better to borrow from a different source.

Chapter 7

Figuring Out Prices and Predicting Sales

. . . .

In This Chapter

▶ Evaluating pricing strategies

▶ Mixing pricing strategies to capture wider markets

▶ Applying price strategies to your business

▶ Building an annual sales forecast

. . . .

*I*f you're like most people starting a business, you may be tempted to undercharge for your products or services. Maybe you're unsure how much customers will pay or you're anxious that customers won't value your services. Perhaps you're worried that you won't secure enough business to cover your expenses.

By undercharging, I'm talking about charging less than your customers are willing to pay. Precisely what this amount is can be tricky to judge, especially if you're pricing a service rather than a product. Calculating the value of your skills and expertise through the eyes of a customer is a very subjective process.

In this chapter, I walk you through pricing strategies and how best to go about setting a price for your products or services. I also explain how to create your sales forecast for the next 12 months — one of the fundamental building blocks for any business plan.

Choosing Pricing Strategies

Business educators use a heap of terminology to explain pricing strategies, but essentially any price strategy boils down to one of three things: Cost-based pricing, competitor-based pricing or value-based pricing. In the following sections I explore each strategy in turn.

Setting prices based on costs

Cost-based pricing is where you figure out what it costs you to make a product or provide a service, and then you add an additional amount to arrive at the profit you're after.

For example, imagine I decide to start a business selling sunhats at the local markets. The hats cost $8 each to buy, the stall costs $100 rent for the day and I reckon I can sell 50 hats a day. I want to make $250 profit to cover my time, so this means I decide to charge $15 per hat. (Sales of $15 × $50 = $750; less the $400 for the cost of the hats, less the rent of $100, and I'm left with $250 in my hot, sticky hand.)

This pricing model may sound like perfectly logical, good business practice, but it's not, because this way of working doesn't pause to consider how much customers are actually prepared to pay for these hats. Maybe another stall opposite is selling the self-same hats for only $12. Perhaps the hats are a real bargain and I should be charging $20.

From a strategic perspective, cost-based pricing is the weakest of all business models. On the one hand, if the resulting prices are too high in relation to the competition, the business will flounder; on the other hand, if resulting prices are less than people are prepared to pay, you'll miss out on the possibility of above-average profits.

Setting prices based on competitors

Competitor-based pricing is where you look at what your competitors are charging for similar products or services, and then set your prices accordingly. This pricing strategy is the most common strategy used by business.

As I mention in this chapter's introduction, if you're just starting out in business you may fall foul of the temptation to be cheaper than everyone else. However, unless everyone else in the industry is driving around in sports cars with money to burn, chances are your competitors' prices are at the level they are for a very good reason. Unless you have a competitive advantage that enables you to produce products or provide your services cheaper than your competitors, setting your prices lower than everyone else is likely to lead to poor profitability for you, and is a risky business model.

Instead of trying to undercut competitors, look at the prices your competitors are charging and use this analysis as a reflection of what the market is prepared to pay. Then pitch your pricing accordingly. (For more about identifying your competitive strategy, refer to Chapter 3.)

Setting prices based on perceived value

Value-based pricing is where you reflect on the products or services you provide, look at customer demand, and then set your price according to how much you think customers will be prepared to pay. Here are some examples of value-based pricing:

- ✔ Apple uses value-based pricing for many of its products (sought-after items such as iPads and iPhones), where no direct head-to-head competition exists and customers are prepared to pay premium prices for a brand upon which they place a high value.

- ✔ The stallholders selling umbrellas outside the city train station close to where I live push up the price of umbrellas by $3 or $4 every time it rains. Why? Because customers place a much higher value on staying dry when the rain is bucketing down.

In many ways, value-based pricing represents the essence of good business sense and marketing. After all, how better to set your prices than by judging the maximum that customers are willing to pay? The only tricky thing about value-based pricing is that any judgement is subjective. For example, I love the design and funky look of Apple's gear and will happily pay a premium for a new iPad or shiny iPhone. My son Daniel, however, doesn't place much value on Apple's design and prefers generic products. Therefore, the value Daniel places on an iPad is significantly less than the value I place on the same item.

Building a Hybrid Pricing Plan

So far in this chapter I've been talking about the theory of pricing and different price strategies. However, most successful businesses don't employ a single pricing strategy but instead employ a combination of strategies.

An example is a luxury inner-city hotel. Most of the time, the hotel uses *competitive-based pricing*, setting rates with the awareness of competitors' pricing very much in mind. However, for premium rooms, the hotel uses *value-based pricing*, often improvising rates on the spot according to demand and what it thinks customers will be prepared to pay. Finally, for last-minute rates where the hotel has a bunch of empty rooms to fill close to a cut-off date, the hotel uses *cost-based pricing*, charging just enough above cost to make it worthwhile to fill each room.

Using a combination of pricing strategies is called *hybrid pricing*, and is a key element in any successful business. You can introduce hybrid pricing into your business in a number of ways, whether by premium products, no-frills products, package pricing or differential pricing.

Offering a premium

With hybrid pricing, offering a premium product or service is only part of the picture. The idea is that as well as offering a premium product or service, you also offer a regular product or service. In other words, you target more than one type of customer. Here are some examples:

- ✔ Amazon offers different pricing for freight, depending on how quickly you want your order delivered.

- ✔ My butcher sells two types of minced beef — low-fat and not-so-low fat.

- ✔ The guy who mows our lawns offers two services, charging 'regular' for just mowing lawns and 'premium' for all-grass-edges-trimmed-within-an-inch-of-their-life mowing.

Cutting back the frills

The flipside of premium pricing (refer to preceding section) is *no-frills pricing*. No-frills pricing doesn't necessarily mean inferior quality, but can include things such as off-peak pricing, lower service standards, longer response times or limited availability. For example:

- ✔ Frequent-flyer programs place restrictions on what flights are available for frequent-flyer points.

- ✔ Many gyms offer low-cost membership if you attend outside peak periods.

- ✔ Supermarkets offer generic brands with basic product packaging.

Getting creative with packages

Package pricing, where one product or service is bundled together with something else, is another example of hybrid pricing. Package pricing can include things such as bundling two or more products or services together, offering bonus products and adding extended warranties. Examples of package pricing include

- ✔ A day spa offering a pedicure, waxing and massage as a package.

- ✔ A tourism operator combining flights, accommodation and meals in a package.

- ✔ A club offering a free giveaway of some kind for every membership renewal.

Charging different prices for the same thing

Yet another pricing strategy is to charge different prices for the same thing (this is also known as *differential pricing*). Don't worry, I'm not proposing you breach trade practice guidelines. Instead, I'm talking about charging different prices depending on the quantity ordered, the total size of an order, the costs of shipping to customers, how promptly customers pay, how much the customer orders in the course of a year, and so on.

Differential pricing works really well for almost any business because it enables you to maintain your margins for regular sales, but generate extra income by selling to other customers at a discount. You have so many ways to implement differential pricing that I'm going to spell out how some obvious examples can work:

- ✓ **Pricing based on customer location:** Charging different rates (either for shipping or for on-site service) depending on where the customer is located makes good sense, although you still want to keep your pricing structure pretty simple.

- ✓ **Pricing based on loyalty:** Offering special pricing to customers who are members of your loyalty program or members of an affiliate organisation is a good marketing strategy and rewards customer loyalty.

- ✓ **Pricing based on order size or quantities ordered:** This kind of pricing makes intuitive sense straight off the bat. Almost any business will charge a different price for someone who buys 1,000 units rather than 10. (When you structure pricing according to quantity, this is called *quantity-break pricing.*)

- ✓ **Pricing based on payment terms:** Offering credit terms is expensive, not just in terms of using up working capital but also because of the risk of bad debt. Consider offering higher discounts for payment upfront or payment within seven days.

- ✓ **Pricing based on customer commitment:** Another clever strategy is to offer discount pricing but make the customer jump through hoops to get it. Money-back coupons where you have to post proof of purchase to the supplier, or price-match guarantees, are examples of this kind of pricing.

Forming Your Plan of Attack

Thinking about the pricing strategies I discuss in the first half of this chapter may help spark some new ideas and creative thinking about how you approach pricing your products or services. However, you may be feeling a little overwhelmed and wondering where to start. Here's what to do:

1. **Research what you think customers will be prepared to pay.**

   Investigate what competitors are charging, then think about how your product or service is different and what value customers are likely to place on this difference.

2. **Think about how you could vary your product or service to provide two or three 'levels' of pricing (no-frills, regular and premium).**

   Not every business can offer multi-level pricing (for example, I don't know that I'd seek out a surgeon offering a no-frills service), but you'd be surprised how many types of businesses can. (Refer to the section 'Building a Hybrid Pricing Plan', earlier in this chapter, for more on pricing levels.)

3. **Investigate at least two ways to bundle or package your offering with other products or services.**

   'Getting creative with packages', earlier in this chapter, provides a few ideas on this topic.

4. **Find two or three ways to charge your customers different prices for the same things.**

   This pricing strategy (differential pricing) is probably the most crucial of all. Even if you can't figure out how to have more than one level of pricing, or you can't think of how to create a package, you should be able to incorporate some form of differential pricing in your strategy. 'Charging different prices for the same thing', earlier in this chapter, provides some pointers.

 Although the upside of a hybrid pricing strategy is that you maximise the number of customers you can reach, and hopefully make premium profits on at least some of your sales, you can risk confusing customers if you offer too many options. As your business grows and changes, experiment with different pricing combinations to see what works best and gets the best response from your customers.

Building Your Sales Forecast

After you figure out your pricing strategy (what you intend to charge per hour, per unit or per service rendered), the next step in your business plan is to create a sales forecast for the next 12 months (or, if your business hasn't started yet, create a sales forecast for the first 12 months).

Creating sales forecasts prompts all kinds of questions. If you're charging by the hour, what's a reasonable number of hours to bill each week? If you're selling items, how do you know how many you'll sell? What if you sell lots of different items at different prices? In the following sections I talk about the details behind creating this kind of projection.

Calculating hours in a working week

If your business charges by the hour (maybe you're a bookkeeper, consultant, electrician, music tutor, plumber or some similar business), one of the first questions to answer is how many hours can you reasonably charge for per week, per month or per year.

Here's how you can go about creating your own estimate of maximum billable hours:

1. **Estimate how many days you're going to work each week and how many hours you can realistically charge for each day to arrive at your average number of billable hours per week.**

   When doing this calculation, remember to list billable hours only. Don't include travel time between locations, or time spent running your business (bookkeeping, phone calls, marketing and so on).

2. **Estimate how much holiday time you're going to take (or be forced to take) each year.**

   Include holidays where you go away and breaks where you may be available to work, but you can't. For example, for the music tutor in Table 7-1 I've included 12 weeks against annual holidays, because 12 is the number of weeks of school holidays each year.

   Don't forget to include public holidays. Depending on where you live in the world, public holidays can number 5 to 12 days per year.

3. **Think of what will happen if you get sick.**

   Most people get sick from time to time, and it's realistic to make an allowance for this.

4. **Calculate how many weeks per year you will be able to charge for.**

   In Table 7-1, after taking out holidays, public holidays and sick days, this person can work a full week (that's 24 billable hours) for only 38 weeks of the year. (By contrast, most businesses that aren't dependent on school terms can probably work more weeks per year than this.)

5. **Multiply the number of working weeks per year by the number of weekly billable hours, to arrive at your maximum billable hours per year.**

In Table 7-1, the maximum billable hours for this music tutor equals 38 weeks per year multiplied by 24 hours per week, making a total of 912 hours.

6. **Multiply your maximum billable hours per year by your hourly rate.**

The result? Your maximum possible income per year.

Table 7-1   Calculating Maximum Billable Hours per Year

Number of days per week	4
Average number of billable hours per day	6
Total billable hours per week	**24**
Number of holiday weeks per year	12
Number of public holidays per year, expressed in weeks	1
Number of sick days per year, expressed in weeks	1
Total working weeks per year	38
Maximum possible billable hours per year	**912**
Hourly rate	$60
Maximum possible income per year	**$54,720**

Note: The method shown in Table 7-1 gives you the maximum billable hours per year for an established business. If you're still getting your business up and running, remember that it may take some time until you have enough customers to reach your maximum billable hours.

To apply the maximum billable hours per year method to your own business, go to www.dummies.com/go/ businessplanningessentials, and use the Calculating Billable Hours Excel worksheet.

If your business is primarily labour-based, don't forget to think beyond your own labour, how many hours you can pack into a week and what you can charge for your time. Instead, expand your thinking to include delegating some of the work involved to employees or subcontractors.

Building a plan that involves employees servicing your customers (rather than just you servicing customers) is a vital part of any entrepreneurial conception. For example, don't simply think in terms of how many lawns you can mow, kids you can tutor or companies you can consult to. Instead, picture a team of people mowing lawns, a whole school of tutors or an entire posse of consultants.

Predicting sales for a new business

If your business is new, making an estimate of your first 12 months' sales can be tricky. Maybe people are going to flood through the door, maybe you're going to be a ten-week wonder, or maybe your business will grow steadily and organically over time. However, in order to build a business plan, you do need to make some kind of estimate.

To ensure your sales forecast is as realistic as possible, the more detail you add, the better. Try to slice up sales targets by *market segment*, *product* or *region*:

✔ **Market segment targets:** *Market segment* is a fancy word that really means type of customer or type of work. For example, a building contractor might split his market into new houses and renovations, a musician might split her market into weddings, private functions and pub gigs. A handyman might split his market into private clients and real estate agents.

✔ **Product-based targets:** Product-based targets work best if you sell products rather than services. You can set sales targets according to units sold, or dollars sold, of each product. For example, a car yard could aim to sell at least 20 cars a month, a real estate agent could try to sell five houses every month, and a lawn-mowing business could set sales targets of 80 lawns per month.

✔ **Regional targets:** With regions, you set sales targets according to geographic regions. This works best for slightly larger businesses that typically have a dedicated salesperson or sales team in each region.

If you take on board any of the pricing strategy stuff I talk about earlier in this chapter (refer to 'Building a Hybrid Pricing Plan'), chances are you're going to have a few different prices or packages on the go. Although this can make your sales forecast complicated, remember that the concept is simple: To create a detailed sales forecast, start by itemising the different items that you sell or the different prices that you charge, then make an estimate of weekly sales against each of these categories. Always try to incorporate a decent level of detail into initial sales estimates.

Go to www.dummies.com/go/businessplanningessentials and select the Detailed Sales Forecasts worksheet. You can then adapt any of the business scenarios to fit yours.

Predicting sales for an established business

If you've been running your business for a while, one of the most accurate ways of predicting sales is to analyse your actual sales over the last 12 months, and then build from there. Sure, you may have changed things now — maybe you've switched to a new location, introduced new products or increased your pricing — but, nonetheless, your historical sales results are always going to provide you with the best indicator for future sales.

When basing sales forecasts on historical data, consider the following:

- ✔ When looking at sales figures for previous months, check whether these figures are shown including or excluding sales/consumer tax. (Most salespeople think in terms of the final value of each sale; accountants tend to look at sales figures net of any taxes collected on behalf of the government.)

- ✔ Does your business have significant seasonal variations? If so, have you factored this into your monthly forecasts?

- ✔ If you examine the trends, is the business growing or declining? Ideally, you should analyse trends over two or more years to truly get a sense of what's happening.

- ✔ Have any changes to pricing or product range occurred between last year and this year?

When looking at sales forecasts, also factor in personalities. Salespeople are often very buoyant with their predictions (this optimism tends to be part of the job), while accountants are typically gloom and doom. Hopefully, your business plan can arrive at a happy medium.

Creating Your Month-by-Month Forecast

At the simplest level, creating a forecast for the next 12 months can be as simple as listing the names of the months in one big row across a sheet of paper and writing an estimate underneath each one. However, this method is somewhat unsophisticated, to put it mildly.

Figures 7-1 and 7-2 show two possible formats. In Figure 7-1, I use the example of a kids' party business that offers three kinds of packages at different prices. This level of detail helps keep forecasts realistic — for example, the business owner in this example can see how many parties they need to do during the month to meet expected sales. In Figure 7-2, I look at a business selling cakes to cafes. The sales projection provides a healthy dose of realism (this business has to sell a lot of friands and muffins to make even the most scant of income at these prices).

	A	B	C	D	E	F
1		Price				
2	1 hour 30 Package	$ 170.00				
3	2 hour Package	$ 190.00				
4	2 hour Plus Package	$ 210.00				
5						
6		Jul-14	Aug-14	Sep-14	Oct-14	Nov-14
7	Parties with owner's labour					
8	1 hour 30 Package	12	12	12	12	12
9	2 hour Package	4	4	4	4	4
10	2 hour Plus Package	1	1	1	1	1
11						
12	Parties with subcontract labour					
13	1 hour 30 Package	8	12	13	8	12
14	2 hour Package	7	6	8	10	12
15	2 hour Plus Package	1	3	4	4	5
16						
17	Income Generated					
18	1 hour 30 Package	$ 3,400	$ 4,080	$ 4,250	$ 3,400	$ 4,080
19	2 hour Package	$ 2,090	$ 1,900	$ 2,280	$ 2,660	$ 3,040
20	2 hour Plus Package	$ 420	$ 840	$ 1,050	$ 1,050	$ 1,260
21	Total Sales	$ 5,910	$ 6,820	$ 7,580	$ 7,110	$ 8,380

Figure 7-1: Building a sales forecast in Excel for a service business.

	A	B	C	D	E	F	G
1		Friands	$ 2.00				
2		Regular Muffins	$ 1.50				
3		Wholesale Muffins	$ 1.30				
4		Chocolate Brownies	$ 2.20				
5		Teacakes	$ 7.00				
10							Sales Fo
11			Jul-14	Aug-14	Sep-14	Oct-14	Nov-14
12		Friands	400	400	420	440	460
13		TOTAL	$ 800	$ 800	$ 840	$ 880	$ 920
15		Regular Muffins	400	400	400	400	400
16		TOTAL	$ 600	$ 600	$ 600	$ 600	$ 600
18		Wholesale Muffins	200	200	200	300	300
19		TOTAL	$ 260	$ 260	$ 260	$ 390	$ 390
21		Chocolate Brownies	520	520	520	520	520
22		TOTAL	$ 1,144	$ 1,144	$ 1,144	$ 1,144	$ 1,144
24		Teacakes	250	250	250	250	250
25		TOTAL	$ 1,750	$ 1,750	$ 1,750	$ 1,750	$ 1,750
27		GRAND TOTAL	$ 4,554	$ 4,554	$ 4,594	$ 4,764	$ 4,804

Figure 7-2: Building a sales forecast in Excel for a business selling products.

For Excel templates that you can adapt to fit your business, go to www.dummies.com/go/businessplanningessentials and look for the Sales Forecast worksheets.

Notice in Figure 7-1 that I separate the services the owners plan to provide themselves, and the services that they plan to use employee or subcontract labour for? I do this because the costs of labour are so different. For example, the owner of the party business does the entertainment at many of the kids' parties herself, and for each of these parties she earns at least $170. However, if she pays someone else to run the party, she earns only $50. Separating out services in this way — analysing what services you'll provide and what services you plan to use subcontractors for — makes good sense so that you can predict costs in the next stage of your business plan (a topic I cover in Chapter 8).

Chapter 8

Calculating Costs and Gross Profit

- -

In This Chapter

▶ Working out the costs for every sale you make

▶ Getting a feel for gross profit and how to crunch the numbers

▶ Focusing on the profit margins for your own business

▶ Creating a gross profit projection for the next 12 months

- -

*T*he summer just past stretched into weeks of long, sunny days. The next-door kids, Callum and Rhys, hatched a plot to make homemade lemonade and sell it to thirsty passers-by. Most days I'd stop and buy a glass and the kids would happily announce how much profit they'd made so far. The school holidays were almost at a close the afternoon I bumped into their mother in the supermarket. She had a trolley piled high with lemons. 'This profit the boys are making is costing me a fortune,' she laughed.

Chances are that such halcyon days belong only to childhood and that, in your business, you want to be seriously realistic about what everything costs. No more lemons for free.

In this chapter, I talk about calculating the costs for each sale that you make, and how to relate these calculations to your gross profit margins. And I show you how to build on your sales projections to include these costs so that you can create a forecast of your gross profit for the year ahead.

Calculating the Cost of Each Sale

The focus of this chapter is the costs that go up and down in direct relation to your sales. For example, if you manufacture wooden tables, your costs include timber. If you sell books, your costs include the purchase of books from publishers.

If you run a small service-based business and you have no employees, you may find that you have no costs of this nature (and, hence, most of this chapter is irrelevant to you). However, before abandoning this chapter willy-nilly, do read through the first couple of sections ('Identifying your variable costs' and 'Costing your service'), just to make sure.

Identifying your variable costs

In order to complete the expenses part of your Profit & Loss Projection for the next 12 months, you first need to grasp the difference between variable costs and fixed expenses. *Variable costs* (also sometimes called *direct costs* or *cost of goods sold*) are the costs that go up and down in direct relation to your sales.

This theory may seem all very well, but you need to understand how it applies in the context of your own business. Here are some examples that may help:

- ✓ If you're a manufacturer, variable costs are the materials you use in order to make things, such as raw materials and production labour. (For the boys next door making lemonade, their variable costs were lemons and sugar.)

- ✓ If you're a retailer, your main variable cost is the costs of the goods you buy to resell to customers. Other variable costs, particularly for online retailers, may include packaging and postage.

- ✓ If you're a service business, you may not have any variable costs, but possible variable costs include sales commissions, booking fees, equipment rental, guest consumables or employee/subcontract labour.

Fixed expenses (also sometimes called *indirect costs* or *overheads*) are expenses that stay constant, regardless of whether your sales go up and down. Typical fixed expenses for your business may include accounting fees, bank fees, computer expenses, electricity, insurance, motor vehicles, rental, stationery and wages.

Not sure which variable costs apply to your business? Figure 8-1 provides a question-based checklist to prompt you to think about your business and what variable costs it may have.

IDENTIFYING VARIABLE COSTS FOR YOUR BUSINESS

Do you use raw materials to create new products?
Examples: Ingredients, foods, timber, metals, plastics, paper

Do you purchase finished products or materials for resale?
Examples: A clothes shop buys clothes, a cafe buys coffee beans, and a landscaper buys soil and plants

Do you purchase any materials for packaging?
Examples: Cardboard, bubble wrap, bottles, caps, envelopes

Do you use any energy as part of manufacturing items?
Examples: Electricity or gas in the factory

Do you employ any labour when manufacturing items?
Examples: Factory wages, subcontractor wages, production wages

Do you employ any labour for which you charge clients or customers directly?
Examples: An electrical company employs electrical contractors and charges customers by the hour for the contractors' time

Do you pay any commissions on sales?
Examples: Sales commission, sales bonuses, sales rebates, sales discounts

Do you have any expenses relating to importing goods from overseas?
Examples: Inwards shipping costs, customs fees, external storage costs

Do you have costs relating to distributing or shipping items?
Examples: Outwards freight, couriers, warehouse rent, warehouse staff

---

Figure 8-1: Identifying variable costs for your business.

Costing your service

I mention near the beginning of this chapter that if you're providing a service, you may not have any variable costs associated with your business. However, you may well have some minor costs associated with providing your service and, as soon as your business grows, you will have the cost of hiring employees or contractors to provide the service on behalf of your business.

Table 8-1 shows some examples where variable costs apply.

Table 8-1 Variable Costs Examples for Service Businesses

Type of Business	Likely Variable Costs
Contract cleaning	Cleaning staff wages, cleaning materials
Holiday house	Guest consumables, booking commissions
Massage therapist	Daily room hire
Home maintenance business	Building materials, cost of subcontractors
Medical practitioner	Medical supplies, pathology

If you're unsure whether something is a variable cost or a fixed expense, ask yourself this: Do you spend more on this item as sales increase? If your answer is yes, chances are this item is a variable cost.

Costing items you buy and sell

When calculating costs for items that you buy and then sell you have two types of costs to consider:

- ✔ **Incoming costs:** These are the costs involved in getting the goods to your door. Incoming costs often include freight and, for importers, may also include customs charges, duties and tax. Incoming costs may also vary significantly depending on the quantity you order.

✔ **Outgoing costs:** These are the costs involved in making the sale and getting the goods to your customer. Outgoing costs include sales commissions, discounts, outwards freight, packaging and storage.

In Table 8-2, I show a costings worksheet for a wholesaler. You can see that, at first glance, the wholesaler's buy price is $9.00 and the sell price is $18.00, making for a handsome margin of 50 per cent. Browse through the figures in more detail, however, allowing for freight, storage, commissions and so on, and you can see that the final margin is something much closer to a paltry 24 per cent. (For more on gross profit and gross profit margin, see 'Understanding Gross Profit', later in this chapter.)

Table 8-2	Calculating True Costs and Margins	
	Percentage of Sell Price	**$**
Sell Price (Before Taxes)		**$18.00**
Less Variable Costs		
Buy price for this item	50%	$9.00
Inwards freight to warehouse	5%	$0.90
Storage costs warehouse	2%	$0.36
Early payment discount	2%	$0.36
Agent commission	10%	$1.80
Outwards freight to customer	6%	$1.08
Packaging	1%	$0.18
Total costs of selling		**$13.68**
Gross Profit		**$4.32**
Gross Profit Margin	**24%**	

If you decide to import goods from overseas, doing your product costings carefully is particularly important. Even if current exchange rates make your prices look cheap as chips, this rosy picture may soon fade when you add the costs of freight, customs, distribution and taxes. Work through your final product costings *before* you consider exporting or importing anything anywhere.

Creating product costings for manufacturers

If you manufacture products, one of the most crucial steps in your business plan is to create an accurate costing worksheet for each product that you sell. This process can be pretty tedious, but without knowing exactly what everything costs, you can't move forward and plan.

Table 8-3 shows a possible product costing and the kind of information to include.

Table 8-3	Cost of Producing One Bottle of Pickles	
Item	**$**	**Notes**
100g fresh tomato	$0.80	Based on seasonal average
30g onion	$0.05	
20g sugar	$0.03	Based on buying in bulk 50 kg bags
5g salt	$0.01	Based on buying in bulk 10 kg bags
Cost of labour	$0.88	Average 400 bottles per day, with labour $350 per day
Kitchen rental	$0.38	Average 400 bottles per day, with rental $150 per day
Bottle plus lid	$0.45	
Label	$0.35	
Packaging	$0.40	$3.20 per custom box, 8 bottles per box
Total	**$3.35**	

Can you see how the example in Table 8-3 puts a value on labour? You may think this doesn't apply to you, because chances are if you're just starting a business you're contributing your own labour for free. However, when creating a product costing, you're best to include a realistic allowance for how much the labour would cost if you were to pay for someone else to create the product. This way, you can see the 'true' profitability of each product, and you get a better sense of the long-term potential of your enterprise.

The other interesting thing to consider is volume discounts. For example, in the product shown in Table 8-3, the cost of sugar is based on buying 50 kilograms at a time. However, how much would this business save if the owner were able to buy 100 kilograms at a time? (Even if your business can't afford to buy in large quantities yet, just knowing that your costs may reduce dramatically as your business grows is an important part of the business planning process.)

Understanding Gross Profit

You've almost certainly heard of the terms *gross profit* or *gross profit margins* but are you entirely clear what these terms mean and why an understanding of these terms is so crucial to your business plan? If you have even a moment's hesitation in answering 'yes' to this question, then read on . . .

Calculating gross profit

Put simply, gross profit is equal to sales less variable costs. A few examples may help bring this concept to life:

- ✔ A fashion retailer buys a skirt from the wholesaler for $20 and sells it for $50. Her gross profit is $30.

- ✔ A massage therapist charges $80 per massage but the therapy centre takes $25 as a booking and room fee. His gross profit is $55.

- ✔ A carpenter charges $800 for fixing a veranda. Materials cost $200 and labour for her apprentice costs $100. Her gross profit is $500.

Sounds okay so far? Just bear in mind:

- ✔ Gross profit equals sales less variable costs

- ✔ Gross profit is always more than net profit

- ✔ The more you sell, the more gross profit you make

Figuring out gross profit margins

Following on from the examples in the preceding section, if a fashion retailer buys a skirt for $20 and sells it for $50, her gross profit is $30. Sounds easy, but how do I figure out her *gross profit margin*? As follows:

> *Gross profit margin* = gross profit divided by sales multiplied by 100

In this example, the retailer's gross profit margin equals $30 divided by $50 (that's gross profit divided by sales) multiplied by 100, which is 60 per cent.

As I mention earlier, the more you sell, the more gross profit you make. However, if your costs stay constant, your gross profit margin stays the same, regardless of how much you sell. For example, if this retailer sells four skirts, her sales would be $200, her costs would be $80, her gross profit would be $120, but her gross profit margin would still be the same, at 60 per cent.

Table 8-4 shows the gross profit and gross profit margins for the three examples from the preceding section.

Table 8-4 Calculating Gross Profit and Gross Profit Margin			
	Fashion Retailer	**Massage Therapist**	**Carpenter**
Sell price	$50.00	$85.00	$800.00
Costs	$20.00	$25.00	$300.00
Gross Profit	$30.00	$60.00	$500.00
Gross Profit Margin	**60%**	**71%**	**63%**

 Unless you know that something cost more to buy or to make than what you sold it for, both your gross profit and your gross profit margin should always be a positive figure.

Looking at margins over time

So far in this chapter, the examples I use talk about gross profit per unit sold or hour worked. However, in real life gross profit margins often vary from one transaction to the next (shopkeepers make a higher margin on gourmet jams than they do on milk, for example).

For this reason, it's good to be able to calculate your average gross profit margins over a period of time. Here's how some different kinds of businesses go about calculating gross profit:

- ✔ A builder constructs a house that then sells for $250,000. He spends $180,000 on materials and labour to build this house. His gross profit on the job is $70,000, and his gross profit margin is 28 per cent.

- ✔ A couple making homemade chilli sauce that they sell in all different shapes and sizes, and at different prices, can see that they made $80,000 in sales over the last 12 months and spent $20,000 on ingredients, bottles, labelling and freight. Their gross profit for the year is $60,000, and their average gross profit margin is 75 per cent.

- ✔ A woman who buys second-hand clothes and resells them on eBay can see that she sold $2,500 on eBay during the month and spent $1,300 on buying clothes and postage. Her gross profit for the month is $1,200, and her average gross profit margin is 48 per cent.

Analysing Margins for Your Business

Have you been reading this chapter and thinking to yourself that this theory is all very well, but you're not a retailer, a carpenter or a massage therapist? If so, never fear. In the following sections I explain how to apply the principles of gross and net profit to your own business.

Calculating margins when you charge by the hour

If you have a service business and you charge by the hour, calculating your gross profit can be blindingly easy. Why? Because sometimes, a service business has no variable costs, and gross profit equals 100 per cent of income. Read on to find out more.

Here's how you work out your gross profit and gross profit margin if you have a service business:

1. **Write down your hourly charge-out rate, not including any taxes that you charge to customers (such as GST, VAT or sales tax).**

2. **Ask yourself whether any variable costs are associated with your service and, if so, calculate how much these costs are per hour.**

   The most likely cost for a service business is employees or subcontract labour. For example, when I ran a contract bookkeeping service, I paid my contractors an hourly rate for doing bookkeeping. This was a variable cost associated with my service.

   If you're a sole owner-operator with no employees, you may find that no variable costs are associated with your service.

3. **Subtract the cost you calculated in Step 2 from the hourly rate from Step 1.**

   This is your gross profit for this service. If you have no variable costs associated with your service, your hourly gross profit is the same as your hourly charge-out rate.

4. **Divide the gross profit you calculated in Step 3 by the hourly rate from Step 1, and divide your result by 100.**

   If you have no variable costs associated with your service, your gross profit margin will be 100 per cent.

5. **Consider the profitability of your service model.**

   Most service businesses need a decent gross profit margin in order to survive. If you're subcontracting out your services, don't underestimate the margin you'll need in order to cover all your business expenses. For example, if you're charging customers $50 per hour but paying employees $35 per hour, leaving yourself with a measly gross profit margin of 30 per cent, you're almost certainly going to be doing things tough.

Calculating margins when you sell products

If you buy or manufacture items that you sell to others, each item has a separate gross profit margin. If you have accounting software and you use this software to track your inventory, you'll be able to generate reports that calculate gross profit margins for you. However, if you don't have this resource, grab a calculator and work through the following for each item you sell:

1. **Write down the sell price of this item, not including any taxes that you charge to customers (such as GST, VAT or sales tax).**

   If the sell price varies depending on the customer, do the analysis for each price you sell this item for.

2. **Write down the cost of this item.**

   If you buy this item from someone else, write down the total cost of purchasing this item, including freight but not including any taxes that you can claim back from the government (such as GST or VAT). If you manufacture this item, write down the total cost of all materials and production labour.

3. **Subtract the cost you calculated in Step 2 from the sell price you calculated in Step 1.**

   This is your gross profit for this item.

4. **Divide the gross profit you calculated in Step 3 by the sell price you calculated in Step 1, and divide your result by 100.**

5. **Consider the results and your fate in life.**

   Number crunching is not an end in itself. Does this margin seem reasonable? If you're not sure, ask around other people who work in the same industry as yourself, and try to get a sense of what margins you should expect.

Always bear in mind that, as long as your pricing policies remain consistent, your gross profit margin should stay relatively constant, no matter how much you sell.

Calculating margins if you do big projects

If you do lots of big projects over the course of a year — maybe you're a builder, you do custom manufacturing or big contract consultancy jobs — you're going to find it tricky to calculate

your hourly gross profit, or your gross profit per unit sold.
A different tack is required:

1. **Look at your total sales for 12 months, not including GST.**

   I'm talking about total sales for all the different products that you sell, combined. If you're looking at a Profit & Loss report to get this figure, don't include things such as interest income, or sundry income from services.

2. **Add up your total variable costs for 12 months, not including GST.**

   If you're an owner-operator with no employees running a service business, you may find that no variable costs are associated with your service. Otherwise, if you're unsure how to figure out what your variable costs are, refer to 'Identifying your variable costs', earlier in this chapter.

3. **Subtract the total costs you calculated in Step 2 from the total sales you calculated in Step 1.**

   This is your gross profit for the past 12 months.

4. **Divide the gross profit you calculated in Step 3 by the total sales you calculated in Step 1, and divide your result by 100.**

5. **Review your overall profitability.**

   What makes an acceptable gross profit margin varies from business to business. However, what's important for you is to be aware of your gross profit margin and ensure that it stays consistent over time.

Building Your Gross Profit Projection

In the earlier chapters in this book, I talk about clarifying your business idea and competitive strategies (Chapters 2 and 3), creating a budget for start-up expenses (Chapter 6), and setting prices and creating your first sales projection (Chapter 7). Next on the road map is expanding your sales projection to add an estimate of direct costs so that you can arrive at a projection of your gross profit for the next 12 months.

Note: I'm assuming here that you've already made a stab at predicting sales for the next 12 months. If you haven't, scoot back to Chapter 7 to complete this process. What you're aiming for is a monthly estimate of total sales for the next 12 months. This could be a single total for each month, or you may choose to split sales into several categories.

What you do next depends on what kind of business you're working on.

Simply you

If you have a service business with no employees and no variable costs, financial forecasting is simple. Just enter the heading 'Variable Costs' in your Gross Profit Projection and leave the figures in this row blank. However, note that if you forecast substantial growth for your business, you may not be able to do all the work yourself, and you may need to hire subcontractors or use employee labour. In this case, you'll need to show the variable costs of this labour.

Adding little helpers

If you have a service business and you use employee or subcontract labour, complete your sales projections for the next 12 months, but separate out sales where you're going to do the work, and sales where you'll get employees or subcontractors to do the work.

Figure 8-2 shows an example. The reason you separate the two is because you're going to have variable costs associated with the services that employees or subcontractors provide.

Probably the easiest way to create this projection is to download a Service Business With Employees template from www.dummies.com/go/businessplanningessentials. The template shows how to set up your projections if you run a service business where employees or subcontractors are part of providing the service.

	A	B	C	D	E
1		Price	Cost		
2	1 hour 30 Package	$ 170.00	$ 115.00		
3	2 hour Package	$ 190.00	$ 130.00		
4	2 hour Plus Package	$ 210.00	$ 145.00		
5					
6		Jul-14	Aug-14	Sep-14	Oct-14
7	**Parties with owner's labour**				
8	1 hour 30 Package	12	12	12	12
9	2 hour Package	4	4	4	4
10	2 hour Plus Package	1	1	1	1
11					
12	**Parties with subcontract labour**				
13	1 hour 30 Package	8	12	13	8
14	2 hour Package	7	6	8	10
15	2 hour Plus Package	1	3	4	4
16					
17	**Income Generated**				
18	1 hour 30 Package	$ 3,400	$ 4,080	$ 4,250	$ 3,400
19	2 hour Package	$ 2,090	$ 1,900	$ 2,280	$ 2,660
20	2 hour Plus Package	$ 420	$ 840	$ 1,050	$ 1,050
21	Total Sales	$ 5,910	$ 6,820	$ 7,580	$ 7,110
22					
23	**Costs**				
24	1 hour 30 Package	920	1,380	1,495	920
25	2 hour Package	910	780	1,040	1,300
26	2 hour Plus Package	145	435	580	580
27		1,975	2,595	3,115	2,800
28					
29	Gross Profit	$ 3,935	$ 4,225	$ 4,465	$ 4,310
30					

Figure 8-2: Building a gross profit projection for a service business with employees or subcontractors.

Small-scale productions

By this kind of business, I'm talking about someone who buys or manufactures a few specific products and then resells them. Examples could include someone making homemade jams, a baker selling pastries, a cafe selling a limited range of items or a cabinet-maker producing a limited range of furniture.

To create a Gross Profit Projection for this kind of business, first complete your sales projections for the next 12 months, with a separate row for each product, and then list your variable costs for the same period, again using a separate row for each product.

The easiest way to create this kind of projection is to go to www.dummies.com/go/businessplanningessentials and download the template called Sales Business With Different Products.

More in the mix

Sometimes, the idea with variable costs is that they are a stable percentage of income. For example, if you pay commissions on sales, these commissions are normally a certain percentage. Or if you're a retailer, the cost of the goods you buy is probably a similar percentage of sales each time you make a sale.

If your variable costs are always a pretty stable percentage of sales, the trick is to set up your gross profit projection so that your variable costs calculate automatically. In other words, set up your worksheet so that if you increase sales, variable costs automatically increase as well. You can see an example of how this format works in Figure 8-3.

Go to www.dummies.com/go/businessplanningessentials to download the Gross Profit Projection Many Products worksheet shown in Figure 8-3.

A	B		C		D		E		F
			Average Sell Price		Cost as a % of sales				
1									
2	Full-price books	$	24.99		60%				
3	Remainder books	$	19.99		20%				
4	DVDs	$	17.99		60%				
5	Postage & Packaging				25%				
6									
7									
8			Jul-14		Aug-14		Sep-14		Oct-14
9	Full-price books		400		400		420		440
10	TOTAL	$	9,996	$	9,996	$	10,496	$	10,996
12	Remainder books		400		410		420		430
13	TOTAL	$	7,996	$	8,196	$	8,396	$	8,596
15	DVDs		200		200		200		300
16	TOTAL	$	3,598	$	3,598	$	3,598	$	5,397
18	GRAND TOTAL	$	21,590	$	21,790	$	22,490	$	24,988
19									
20	LESS: VARIABLE COSTS								
21	Full-price books	$	5,998	$	5,998	$	6,297	$	6,597
22	Remainder books	$	1,599	$	1,639	$	1,679	$	1,719
23	DVDs	$	2,159	$	2,159	$	2,159	$	3,238
24	Postage & Packaging	$	5,398	$	5,447	$	5,622	$	6,247
25	TOTAL VARIABLE COSTS	$	15,153	$	15,243	$	15,758	$	17,802
26									
27	GROSS PROFIT	$	6,437	$	6,547	$	6,732	$	7,187
28									

Figure 8-3: Building a gross profit projection for a business selling lots of different kinds of products, or calculating costs on a percentage basis.

Chapter 9

Planning for Expenses

In This Chapter

▶ Creating a 12-month forecast for business expenses

▶ Tweaking your forecast so it's as accurate as can be

▶ Understanding where taxes and loan repayments fit

▶ Assessing your personal budget

*A*lthough a business plan takes many shapes and sizes, pretty much every business plan includes a projection of both income and expenses for the next 12 months ahead. (Some business plans extend further than this, for three or even five years; however, for most purposes, 12 months usually does just fine.)

In this chapter, I focus on the expenses side of this 12-month forecast. Estimating future expenses isn't some idle form of crystal-ball gazing where you pluck some figures out of the air until you arrive at a final prediction of profit that makes you sleep easy. Instead, planning each expense in detail provides you with an opportunity for a reality check, even if this reality can prove rather chilling at times.

I also suggest that if you're creating your first business plan, you look at not only your likely business expenses for the next 12 months, but also your personal expenses. After all, in the absence of benevolent fairy godmothers or inheritances from wealthy great-aunties, starting a business that requires your full-time input but doesn't generate enough profits for you to survive is never going to fly.

Concentrating on Expenses

I accept that this book provides no gripping plot, murders or sex scenes, and that few people picking up this book are going to start at Chapter 1 and read through to the end. Instead, you're probably flicking through pages, picking and choosing the bits you're interested in, which is generally okay. However, when you're working on financial projections, simply jumping in at whatever chapter catches your eye can be a time-wasting exercise.

As I explain in Chapter 1, the typical financial planning cycle involves creating a start-up budget, followed by estimating prices, costs and expenses. You then use this information to create Profit & Loss Projections, break-even analysis reports and Cashflow Projections.

If you've been working through this cycle chapter by chapter, you'll be about halfway through this process. (Chapter 6 focuses on budgeting for start-up expenses, Chapter 7 on prices and rates, Chapter 8 on product costs and gross profit and Chapter 9 — that's this chapter — on expense budgets. Chapter 10 then completes your Profit & Loss Projection.)

So, if you've just picked up this book and plunged in at this chapter, pause for a moment and check that you've already covered the initial stages of your financial plan (that is, creating a start-up budget, setting prices and calculating product costs). If you haven't, take the time to get these foundations in place first.

Separating start-up expenses from other expenses

When planning for business expenses, always separate *start-up expenses* from *ongoing expenses*:

- ✔ *Start-up expenses* are one-off expenses you encounter when you first start a business, such as new equipment, company formation expenses, legal expenses and signage. I talk lots about start-up expenses in Chapter 6.

- ✔ *Ongoing expenses* are the kind of expenses that occur year in and year out, and which form a regular part of everyday trading. Ongoing expenses are the focus of the next part of this chapter.

When you're working with Profit & Loss Projections in your business plan, you only include ongoing expenses. Start-up expenses — if relevant to you — are shown separately.

Similarly, remember the difference between *variable costs* and *fixed expenses*.

> ✔ *Variable costs* (also sometimes called *direct costs* or *cost of goods sold*) are the costs that go up and down in direct relation to your sales.

> ✔ *Fixed expenses* (also sometimes called *indirect costs* or *overheads*) are expenses that stay constant, regardless of whether your sales go up and down.

This chapter focuses on fixed expenses only. For more about creating a worksheet that forecasts variable costs, refer to Chapter 8.

Thinking of what expenses to include

If you've been running your business for a while, you already have a good idea of what your expenses for the next 12 months are going to be. However, if you're just getting started with your business plan, thinking of the types of expenses you may encounter can be tricky. Are you going to take out insurance? What about accounting fees? Will you need to pay any professional memberships? What expenses could you face that you haven't even thought of yet?

Figure 9-1 shows a Business Expenses worksheet that lists expenses in the first column, how often they occur in the second column and an estimate of the amount in the third. The monthly total shown in the fourth column calculates automatically. You can download this worksheet from www.dummies.com/go/businessplanningessentials.

Here's how to make use of the Business Expenses worksheet:

1. **Go to www.dummies.com/go/businessplanningessentials and download the Business Expenses worksheet template. Save this onto your computer, then open it in Excel.**

   You can also open up this template in most other spreadsheet software, if you prefer.

2. **For each expense account, make a stab at how much you think this expense will be for your business, and whether this expense occurs weekly, fortnightly, quarterly, monthly or annually.**

   If your business is already trading, the best way to make estimates is to look at what you've spent in the past. Old supplier invoices, accounting software transaction journals and monthly Profit & Loss Statements are all good sources for this information.

   Round all amounts to the nearest $20 or so — forecasts aren't meant to be a science.

3. **Delete any expenses that aren't relevant to your business.**

   The list of expenses in this worksheet is pretty comprehensive, so you'll almost certainly find that some of these expenses aren't relevant to you. Where that's the case, simply delete that row in the worksheet. (Highlight the row, right-click with your mouse, then select Delete.)

4. **Add any expenses that are relevant to your business but aren't included on this list.**

   To insert a row, right-click where you want the row to be, select Insert, then Entire Row.

   Don't insert any variable costs (costs of purchasing goods for resale, or costs of production). What you're focusing on in this chapter is fixed expenses only. (For more about variable costs, refer to Chapter 8.)

5. **Check that the monthly estimates for each expense make sense.**

   Excel automatically calculates how much each expense will cost every month, depending on the frequency you select. At this point, look at these calculations and see if they make sense to you.

6. **Review the totals at the bottom of the Monthly Total column.**

   The Total Expenses row automatically adds up all the rows above it. This means that if you change a figure, the total recalculates automatically.

   To get a spreadsheet to do this calculation, you have to insert a formula. In Excel, the easiest way to do this is to press your AutoSum button (the one with a Greek

	A	B	C	D
7	**Type of Expense**	**Freqency**	**Estimate**	**Monthly total**
8	Accounting Fees	Annually	$1,500	$125
9	Advertising	Monthly	$1,200	$1,200
10	Bank Charges	Monthly	$100	$100
11	Cleaning Expenses	Weekly	$50	$217
12	Computer Consumables	Monthly	$150	$150
13	Consultant Expenses	Monthly	$300	$300
14	Couriers	Monthly	$80	$80
15	Customer Consumables	Monthly	$60	$60
16	Electricity	Quarterly	$500	$167
17	Equipment Rental	Monthly	$200	$200
18	Freight Fees	Monthly	$300	$300
19	Gas	Quarterly	$300	$100
20	Hire Purchase Payments	Monthly	$650	$650
21	Insurance	Annually	$3,000	$250
22	Interest Expense	Monthly	$520	$520
23	Internet Fees	Monthly	$150	$150
24	Lease Expenses	Monthly	$800	$800
25	License Fees	Annually	$1,200	$100
26	Merchant Fees	Monthly	$320	$320
27	Motor Vehicle rego & insurance	Annually	$1,500	$125
28	Motor Vehicle Fuel	Weekly	$80	$347
29	Motor Vehicle Repairs & Maint	Annually	$2,000	$167
30	Motor Vehicle Tolls	Weekly	$70	$303
31	Office Supplies	Monthly	$150	$150
32	Parking	Weekly	$35	$152
33	Professional Memberships	Annually	$1,800	$150
34	Rates	Quarterly	$400	$133
35	Rental Expense	Fortnightly	$1,500	$3,250
36	Repairs and Maintenance	Annually	$6,000	$500
37	Replacements	Annually	$3,000	$250
38	Security Expenses	Monthly	$120	$120
39	Staff Amenities	Monthly	$300	$300
40	Storage Expenses	Monthly	$150	$150
41	Subcontractor Expenses	Monthly	$520	$520
42	Subscription and Dues	Annually	$2,200	$183
43	Telephone (inc mobile)	Monthly	$550	$550
44	Travel Domestic	Monthly	$350	$350
45	Travel Overseas	Annually	$3,500	$292
46	Wages and Salaries	Weekly	$3,500	$15,167
47	Wages oncosts	Weekly	$350	$1,517
48	Website expenses	Monthly	$850	$850
49	**Total Expenses**			**$29,672**

Figure 9-1: In this Business Expenses worksheet, start by estimating an amount for each expense, along with how often it occurs.

symbol that looks a bit like an 'E'). However, if you're using the template downloaded from www.dummies. com/go/businessplanningessentials, this formula is already there.

7. **Ignore the figures in the individual month columns.**

   I talk more about these in the following section.

Building a 12-month projection

Figure 9-2 shows an example of possible expenses for a relatively small business. You can see the months running along the top, the names of the expenses down the first column, and an estimate of how much each expense will be along each row.

Looks good? Then it's time for you to give it a go:

1. **Open up your Business Expenses worksheet.**

   Refer to the preceding section for more on this worksheet. Hopefully you've already completed the first three columns of this worksheet, and added or deleted expense accounts so that this worksheet is relevant for your business.

2. **Change the names on the months along the top row.**

   My example has January as the first month, but obviously you're going to start with the month that corresponds to the period of your business plan. For example, if you plan to open in August, August is going to be the first month in this worksheet.

3. **Complete dollar estimates for expenses, month by month.**

   If the template is working as it should, the monthly estimates will appear automatically (and correctly) for all weekly, fortnightly or monthly expenses. However, with expenses that you pay out only quarterly or annually, you'll need to change the amounts so that they fall in the right months. For example, in the Accounting Fees row at the top, I have a single amount in October, when these fees normally fall due. (To make this change, I simply scroll across this row, deleting the monthly amounts, and type the whole year's allocation into the October column.)

If you use accounting software, you may be able to export a month-by-month summary of all expenses out of your accounting software and into Excel. If you think that your expenses are likely to be similar in the next 12 months to what they were in the previous 12 months, this method provides a quick and efficient way to populate the amounts in your Business Expenses worksheet.

4. Have a further think about the nature of annual expenses.

You'll find some expenses occur only once a year (such as accounting fees or membership dues). For these expenses you can simply enter the whole budget for the year in the month when payment is going to fall due.

For other expenses, however, you may have an idea of how much the annual total will be, but you don't know when payment will be due. Vehicle repairs are a good example. I know that my car usually clocks in at approximately $2,000 of repairs per year, but I never know when these bills are going to fall due. With these kinds of expenses, I just enter an annual estimate (as you can see I do in row 29 of Figure 9-2), and leave a monthly amount in place.

5. Check the formula for Total Expenses.

The idea of the Total Expenses row is that it automatically adds up all the rows above it. To get your spreadsheet to do this calculation you have to insert a formula. In Excel, the easiest way to do this is to press your AutoSum button (the one with a Greek symbol that looks a bit like an 'E').

This formula is already in the Business Expenses template, but if you've inserted or deleted rows, you may have knocked it out of whack. Click on the formula and check it still makes sense. (For example, **=SUM(G12:G48)** means that Excel is going to add up every figure from cell G12 down to cell G48.)

6. Save your work and ponder.

With your final worksheet complete, spend a generous amount of time checking it over, ensuring it makes sense and is realistic.

Type of Expense	Freqency	Estimate	Monthly total	Jan	Feb	Mar	Apr
Accounting Fees	Annually	$1,500	$125	$1,500	$0	$0	$0
Advertising	Monthly	$1,200	$1,200	$1,200	$1,200	$1,200	$1,200
Bank Charges	Monthly	$100	$100	$100	$100	$100	$100
Cleaning Expenses	Weekly	$50	$217	$217	$217	$217	$217
Consultant Expenses	Monthly	$300	$300	$300	$300	$300	$300
Customer Consumables	Monthly	$60	$60	$60	$60	$60	$60
Electricity	Quarterly	$500	$167	$500			$500
Freight Fees	Monthly	$300	$300	$300	$300	$300	$300
Gas	Quarterly	$300	$100		$300		
Insurance	Annually	$3,000	$250				
Interest Expense	Monthly	$520	$520	$520	$520	$520	$520
Internet Fees	Monthly	$150	$150	$150			$150
Lease Expenses	Monthly	$800	$800	$800	$800	$800	$800
Motor Vehicle rego & insurance	Annually	$1,500	$125				
Motor Vehicle Fuel	Weekly	$80	$347	$347	$347	$347	$347
Motor Vehicle Repairs & Maint	Annually	$2,000	$167	$167	$167	$167	$167
Office Supplies	Monthly	$150	$150	$150	$150	$150	$150
Parking	Weekly	$35	$152	$152	$152	$152	$152
Professional Memberships	Annually	$1,800	$150		$1,800		
Rates	Quarterly	$400	$133	$400			$400
Rental Expense	Fortnightly	$1,500	$3,250	$3,250	$3,250	$3,250	$3,250
Repairs and Maintenance	Annually	$6,000	$500	$500	$500	$500	$500
Replacements	Annually	$3,000	$250	$250	$250	$250	$250
Subcontractor Expenses	Monthly	$520	$520	$520	$520	$520	$520
Telephone (inc mobile)	Monthly	$550	$550	$550	$550	$550	$550
Travel Domestic	Monthly	$350	$350	$350	$350	$350	$350
Wages and Salaries	Weekly	$850	$15,167	$15,167	$15,167	$15,167	$15,167
Wages oncosts	Weekly	$85	$1,517	$1,517	$1,517	$1,517	$1,517
Website expenses	Monthly	$850	$850	$850	$850	$850	$850
Total Expenses			$28,466	$29,816	$29,366	$27,266	$28,316

Figure 9-2: Forecasting expenses for the months ahead.

Finetuning Your Worksheet

With the first draft of your expenses worksheet complete, you're ready to finetune it so you can be sure that your projections are as accurate as possible. Look at relationships between expenses, think about irregular payments and focus on large expenses in a bit more detail.

Recognising relationships

One important thing to muse over is whether any expense categories are directly related to one another. For example, staff oncosts such as insurance or superannuation usually go up or down in direct proportion to wages.

The trick is to tell your spreadsheet about relationships so that it calculates them for you automatically. In Figure 9-2, for example, you can see a figure for wages in row 34. I know that wages oncosts average 10 per cent of wages, so my formula for wages oncosts is =**C34*10%**. The neat thing about specifying relationships in this way is that when you change one figure in the spreadsheet, other figures change automatically, too.

Allowing for irregular payments

When creating expense projections, take a while to consider expenses that vary from month to month or change with the seasons. Here are a few specifics to consider:

✔ Fuel bills, such as electricity and gas, often fall due every two or three months, rather than every month.

✔ If you pay wages every week, bear in mind that every third month you'll get a month with five paydays, not four.

✔ Think about seasonal variations. Depending on your business, expenses can increase or decrease dramatically at different times of year.

✔ If you're a small owner-operated business, think about when you may take holidays, and whether you need to increase your wages expense during this time.

Playing the 10 per cent rule

I have a technique that I've developed over the years as a way of ensuring that my expense estimates are more likely to be accurate. What I do is go through the worksheet and identify any expenses that make up more than 10 per cent of the total expenses. For example, if you look at Figure 9-2, you can see that wages make up almost 50 per cent of total expenses. For such a small business, this wages bill makes up a huge proportion of outgoings.

If your expenses worksheet includes any one expense that's more than 10 per cent of total expenses, see if you can split this expense up in more detail. In the example shown in Figure 9-2, I would suggest to the business that they add more detail about wages in the worksheet — for example, listing each staff member separately, or listing each category of wages separately.

Thinking about Taxes and Loan Repayments

In the following sections, I touch on some of the pain points that you're likely to encounter at this stage of your plan, hopefully supplying straightforward answers to some of the more complicated of questions.

Allowing for personal and company tax

One of the questions people often ask is whether to include personal or company tax in the worksheet. The answer depends on whether your business is structured as a sole trader, partnership or company.

If you're a sole trader or partnership, you're responsible for paying tax on any profit that the business makes. The amount of tax you pay depends on many factors, including whether you have any sources of income other than the business. Generally, I don't include personal income tax as an expense on any business plan.

If your business has a company structure, you do need to include company tax expense on your expenses worksheet. In Chapter 10, I explain how to pull all the different elements of your business plan together, starting with your income worksheet, deducting your cost of sales and business expenses, calculating net profit, and finally adding two rows called Company Tax Expense, and Net Profit After Company Tax.

Understanding where other taxes fit in

What about taxes such as sales tax, VAT or GST? The answer depends on where you live.

If your business is subject to any kind of value-added tax (known, for example, as VAT in Canada and the United Kingdom, or GST in Australia and New Zealand), you don't include this tax in any of your expenses. Instead, you show the value of each expense before tax is applied. (Why? Because this kind of tax applies only to the final sale to the consumer — as a business, you're entitled to claim back any tax of this nature that you pay.) On the other hand, if your business pays a sales tax (something that applies in almost every state within the United States), you should include sales tax in your expenses, showing the value of each expense inclusive of the tax that you pay. (Why? Because this tax forms part of the cost of this expense — you can't claim this tax back from the government.)

Dealing with loan repayments and interest

If your business has borrowed money and you're paying off a business loan, deciding how to show loan repayments in your expenses worksheet can be quite tricky.

Imagine that you have a bank loan and your repayments are $1,000 per week. You've almost paid off this loan, and you currently have only $15,000 left to repay. The interest on this loan equals only about $15 per week.

Any accountant will gladly explain that in terms of the profit of your business, the only expense that you can claim is the interest. However, when you're doing a business plan, this kind of analysis is too simplistic. The interest may be inconsequential, but budgeting $1,000 a week in repayments is not.

The best way to show loan repayments in your business plan depends on the circumstances:

- If you decide to include both a Profit & Loss Projection and a Cashflow Projection in your business plan (and if you're not sure yet, skip ahead to Chapter 10), you should show the value of the interest expense in your Profit & Loss Projection, and the value of the whole loan repayment in your Cashflow Projection.

- If your business plan only requires a Profit & Loss Projection, stay on the side of caution and show the full value of the loan repayment in your expenses worksheet. This way, the final net profit that you arrive at in your projections will be as close as possible to your likely surplus in cash.

Factoring in Personal Expenses

If you're starting a new business and you have very little savings or start-up capital, you may find you don't have much to live on while building up your business. In this scenario, I can't stress enough how important it is to create a budget not only for business expenses, but also for personal expenses.

Even if your business is already up and running, creating a budget for personal expenses is usually still a good idea. You must ensure that your business is going to generate enough income to cover your personal expenses. If not, you may need to make changes to your business plan (such as adjusting expenses or increasing income) or, alternatively, make some changes to your personal spending patterns.

I've created a template in Excel that you can use as a starting point for your personal budget. To access the Personal Expenses worksheet, go to www.dummies.com/go/ businessplanningessentials.

Chapter 10

Assembling Your Profit & Loss Projection

- -

In This Chapter

▶ Getting acquainted with some spreadsheet theory

▶ Arriving at the moment of truth: Your 12-month Profit & Loss Projection

▶ Determining your net profit and rate of return

▶ Looking at scenario analysis, cashflows and other financial reports

- -

*I*n this chapter I pull together all the information that goes into a Profit & Loss Projection, including pricing and sales projections, costs and gross profit projections and expense projections. This helps you arrive at an estimate of just how much profit your business is likely to generate over the next 12 months.

Looking at your likely profits can be an emotional turning point, especially if this is the first Profit & Loss Projection you've ever made. Few people go into business without wanting to make a profit and, if the Profit & Loss Projection shows limited profits for what's likely to be a heap of work, you'll probably feel rather discouraged.

Feeling discouraged is okay. If your business model is a dud, you're better to quit now while you're ahead than spend a year or two on an idea that will never fly. On the other hand, if you suspect that your essential idea is still strong, this part of the planning process gives you another chance to look at all your figures and experiment with pricing, costs and expenses.

Of course, you may find that your financial projections predict a business with a rosy future. So long as you take any figures that seem overly optimistic with a pinch of salt, you're off to a flying start.

Understanding More About Spreadsheets

Last year, we had a young visitor from overseas stay with us. One evening, she talked about the sports education at her very traditional school. It turned out that after six years of high school education she knew the dimensions of a soccer, basketball or cricket field by heart, as well as the number of players and the rules involved in each sport. Yet she had never once kicked a ball, scored a goal or wielded a cricket bat.

This kind of education seems daft to me, in the same way that explaining the theory of financial projections without talking about spreadsheets also seems daft. A spreadsheet is the only viable tool for creating financial projections, and to pretend otherwise is simply to make the job harder than it needs to be.

I don't have enough space here to discuss the technicalities of using spreadsheets, but I have created a series of Excel how-to videos, all aimed at explaining simple techniques that help when creating your business plan. I cover the topics of how to add up columns, apply formatting, create graphs, freeze rows and columns, link worksheets, name cells and use conditional highlighting. To view these videos, go to www.dummies.com/go/businessplanningessentials.

Building Your Profit & Loss Projection

Ready to create your first Profit & Loss Projection for the next 12 months? Then make yourself a hot cup of something and get set to see how all the bits of your plan fit together.

Step one: Projected sales

The top of any Profit & Loss Projection always starts by showing income, then cost of sales, then gross profit. I talk about calculating gross profit in detail in Chapter 8, so if you haven't already worked through your Gross Profit Projections, scoot to Chapter 8 first. With these workings in place, you're ready to go:

1. **Using Excel (or any other spreadsheet software), open up your Gross Profit Projection worksheet.**

   Refer to Chapter 8 for more about this worksheet. The idea is that you've already created a worksheet estimating both your sales and your cost of sales for the next 12 months.

2. **Rest your mouse on the tab at the bottom of this worksheet that says Sheet1 and right-click.**

   Are you using a Macintosh with no right-click button on the mouse? Don't worry. Instead, press the Control button and then click the mouse.

3. **Click Rename and then type GrossProfit as the name.**

4. **Rest your mouse on the tab that says Sheet2 and right-click.**

5. **Rename this tab to become ProfitLoss.**

   You have now created and named two separate worksheets within a workbook. The first worksheet is called GrossProfit and the second worksheet is called ProfitLoss.

6. **On the second worksheet, label the months along the top (in row 1).**

7. **Go to your GrossProfit tab and highlight the row where you recorded the grand total for sales each month, right-click with your mouse, then select Copy.**

   Or, if you're using a Mac, hold down the Control button and then click.

8. **Return to the ProfitLoss tab and click on cell B2.**

   Cell B2 is where the first month of total sales is going to show.

9. **Right-click and select Paste Special.**

10. **Click the Paste Link button that appears in the bottom-left of this dialogue box.**

    Before your eyes, the sales for each month should appear right across row 2, similar to Figure 10-1. (I just show the first few months here, but you get the general idea.)

⊿	A	B	C	D	E	F	G	⊟
1		July	Aug	Sep	Oct	Nov	Dec	
2	Total Sales	31,070	35,440	41,150	36,450	47,260	174,890	1
3	✎							
4								

⟨ ◀ ▶ ▶⟩ GrossProfit ╱ **ProfitLoss** ╱ Sheet3 ╱ 🎧 ╱

Figure 10-1: Total sales form the first line of your Profit & Loss Projection.

Are you wondering why I've gone to all the trouble of creating multiple worksheets and linking one sheet to another, rather than just copying and pasting the estimated total sales? The reason I suggest you work this way is so that your total sales will update automatically whenever you tweak your detailed sales. For example, maybe I want to see what would happen if I lift my pricing by 10 per cent. All I have to do is tweak the sales figures in my Gross Profit Projection worksheet and this change flows automatically through to my Profit & Loss Projection.

Of course, if you're a very small business and you don't want to go to the trouble of splitting up your income in any kind of detail — you just want to type in an estimated dollar total for each month — then you don't need to bother creating a separate worksheet for sales projections.

Step two: Variable costs

You need to complete your gross profit projections before you do this step. If you haven't, check out the last few pages of Chapter 8 before continuing.

1. **Go to the GrossProfit tab, and highlight the rows where you recorded the total for cost of sales and gross profit for each month. Right-click with your mouse (or press Control then click if you're on a Mac) and select Copy.**

2. **Return to the ProfitLoss tab and click on cell A4.**

3. **Right-click and select Paste Special.**

4. **Click the Paste Link button that appears in the bottom-left of this dialogue box.**

   Your total cost of sales for each month, as well as Gross Profit, should now appear below your sales. (If a bunch of zeros appear in row 5, which may happen because row 5 is blank in the Gross Profit worksheet, simply delete these zeros.)

5. **Format the cells if necessary.**

Sometimes the formatting doesn't come across correctly. So feel free to add bold to your headings and format amounts to include dollar signs.

6. **Check your results.**

By the time you're done, your worksheet should look similar to Figure 10-2, showing total sales, cost of sales and gross profit for the next 12 months. This worksheet has exactly the same figures as your gross profit projection, but with the difference that it displays much less detail. This less detailed format is what many investors or bank managers would expect to see as an overall financial projection.

	A	B	C	D	E	F	G	
1		July	Aug	Sep	Oct	Nov	Dec	
2	Total Sales	31,070	35,440	41,150	36,450	47,260	174,890	
3								
4	Total Cost of Sales	19,095	22,035	25,930	22,780	30,125	116,560	
5								
6	Gross Profit	11,975	13,405	15,220	13,670	17,135	58,330	
7								

GrossProfit ProfitLoss Sheet3

Figure 10-2: Cost of sales and gross profit show below total sales on your Profit & Loss Projection.

Step three: Expenses budget

Step three in building your Profit & Loss Projection is to add detail regarding your expenses. Chapter 9 explains how to create a worksheet that accurately forecasts business expenses on a monthly basis, and I'm going to assume here that you've already completed this worksheet.

Here's how to add expenses to your Profit & Loss Projection:

1. **With your Profit & Loss Projection workbook open, right-click the tab called Sheet3, select Rename and call this tab Expenses.**

With the instructions on the next page or two, I often tell you to right-click with your mouse. But if you're one of those sensible people who use a Mac, instead press the Control button and then click.

2. **Open up your expenses worksheet.**

Refer to Chapter 9 for details on how to create this spreadsheet.

3. **Highlight every single cell that has anything in it.**

   In other words, click in the top-left cell and drag your mouse down to the bottom-right cell.

4. **Right-click and select Copy.**

5. **Go to your Profit & Loss Projection workbook and click the Expenses tab.**

6. **Go to the top-left cell in this worksheet, then right-click and select Paste.**

   Cool. You've just copied everything from your expenses worksheet into your Profit & Loss worksheet. All good so far.

7. **Now highlight the names of the expenses in Column A, right-click and select Copy.**

   I'm just talking the labels of your expenses here, such as Accounting Fees and Advertising Expenses.

8. **Go to the ProfitLoss tab, click cell A8 and select Paste Special, followed by Paste Link.**

   What you're doing here is linking the list of expenses in your Expenses Worksheet to the list of expenses in your Profit & Loss Projection.

9. **Back on the Expenses tab, highlight the total value for each month, right-click and select Copy.**

10. **Go to the ProfitLoss tab of your worksheet, click cell B8 and select Paste Special, followed by Paste Link.**

    There you have it. You now have a Profit & Loss worksheet that starts with sales, then shows cost of sales and gross profit, and finally lists all your expenses. Figure 10-3 shows how these expenses come across (although for the sake of fitting everything onto the page, I've hidden some of the expense rows).

Are you wondering why I suggest you copy across all the expense totals from your worksheet, rather than just a single total for expenses in the same way as you did for sales and cost of sales? The reason is partly historical. Accountants, bank managers and investors are accustomed to a standard format for Profit & Loss Projections, and this format typically provides a summary of sales and cost of sales, and more detail for expenses.

	A	B	C	D	E
1		July	Aug	Sep	Oct
2	Total Sales	31,070	35,440	41,150	36,450
3					
4	Total Cost of Sales	19,095	22,035	25,930	22,780
5					
6	Gross Profit	11,975	13,405	15,220	13,670
7					
8	Accounting Fees	-	-	-	-
9	Advertising	1,200	1,200	1,200	1,200
10	Bank Charges	100	100	100	100
11	Cleaning Expenses	217	217	217	217
12	Computer Consumables	150	150	150	150
13	Consultant Expenses	300	300	300	300
14	Couriers	80	80	80	80
43	Telephone (inc mobile)	550	550	550	550
44	Travel Domestic	350	350	350	350
45	Travel Overseas	-	-	-	-
46	Wages and Salaries	3,683	3,683	3,683	3,683
47	Wages oncosts	368	368	368	368
48	Website expenses	850	850	850	850
49	Total Expenses	17,340	17,490	15,890	16,440
50					
51	Net Profit	- 5,365	- 4,085	- 670	- 2,770

Figure 10-3: Your completed Profit & Loss Projection.

Step four: The bottom line

The next step in building your 12-month Profit & Loss Projection is the easiest of all — calculating net profit.

Net profit is simply your gross profit less your expenses. So all you have to do is add a line that says Net Profit at the bottom of your worksheet, and insert a formula that subtracts Total Expenses from Gross Profit. In Figure 10-3, the formula for July's net profit would be =**B6-B49**. Your formula will be different because you're bound to have a different number of rows for your expenses, but I'm sure you get the general idea.

Notice that in Figure 10-3, I also added a final column showing the total for each row, so that I can see the total sales, gross profit, expenses and net profit for the whole 12 months combined.

Step five: Tax, glorious tax

If you're a sole trader or partnership, the amount of personal tax you pay depends on many factors, including whether you have any other sources of income other than the business. For this reason, I suggest that you don't include personal income tax as an expense on your Profit & Loss Projection, but that you make an allowance for tax when calculating how much you require in personal drawings. (See the section 'Assessing whether your net profit is reasonable, or not'.)

However, if your business has a company structure, you need to include company tax as an expense on your Profit & Loss Projection based on the profits you make. To do this, simply add a final line to your Profit & Loss report called Company Tax Expense. Calculate this expense at the correct percentage of company tax and then add a final line to your worksheet called Net Profit After Tax. Figure 10-4 shows an example, with the company tax rate calculated at 30 per cent.

54	Net Profit	$	8,467	$	11,374	$	16,652	$	12,909	$	20,989	$	109,372
55													
56	Company Tax Expense	$	2,540	$	3,412	$	4,995	$	3,873	$	6,297	$	32,811
57													
58	Net Profit After Tax	$	5,927	$	7,962	$	11,656	$	9,036	$	14,692	$	76,560

Figure 10-4: Adding an extra line to show company tax.

Checking you've got it right

You're not quite done yet. The last step is to check that you got everything right. (Spreadsheets are great in the way they calculate everything for you, but get one formula wrong, and the error can spread like a naked celebrity shot on Twitter.)

So here's your checklist:

✔ Save your workings and then re-open your Gross Profit Projection worksheet. Temporarily change your prices to $10 for every product, change your unit costs to $1, and change the unit sales to 100 units per month. Check that your gross profit comes out at $900 every month. Then quit without saving.

✔ Grab a calculator and manually check the sums for the first and the last month in your forecast. Check total sales, gross profit, total expenses and net profit.

✔ If your business is already up and running, print out your Profit & Loss report for the most recent month. Plug in the figures from this report into the first month of your Profit & Loss Projection and check that the net profit in your projection matches with the report.

All good? Then you're ready to move on to the next part of your business plan, where you get to ponder whether the forecasted profit is what you need it to be . . .

Analysing Net Profit

As I mention in the preceding section, one of the primary purposes of your Profit & Loss Projection is to figure out how much profit you'll be left with at the end of the day. This result enables you to decide whether you want to continue with this business, whether you need to change your business model in some way, and whether you're making a reasonable rate of return on your investment.

Calculating net profit margins

So, to do a quick recap:

- ✔ Gross profit equals sales less variable costs.
- ✔ Net profit equals gross profit less fixed expenses.
- ✔ Gross profit is always more than net profit.
- ✔ The more you sell, the more gross profit you make.
- ✔ The more you sell, the more net profit you make.

To calculate your net profit margin, you first calculate your net profit, and then you divide this amount by the value of total sales and multiply the result by 100. For example, if my sales are $200,000 a year and my net profit is $6,000, my net profit margin is 3 per cent (that's $6,000 divided by $200,000 multiplied by 100).

Assessing whether your net profit is reasonable, or not

There is no such thing as a specific percentage rate at which you can say that a net profit margin is reasonable, because too many variables affect this judgement. However, you should be able to establish for yourself a rate that you think is reasonable, and run with that.

The biggest factor to take into account is whether the net profit on your Profit & Loss Projection includes payment for your time. If your business has a sole trader or partnership structure, the final net profit on your Profit & Loss Projection represents the profit that your business generates before you see a single cent in payment for your time. Therefore, the net profit (and hence the net profit margins) need to be much higher than for an equivalent business with a company structure. (In contrast, if your business has a company structure, you need to include your monthly wages as part of your expenses, and so payment for your time is already accounted for.)

Another approach is to think about how much you need to live comfortably. If the net profit of your business is more than what you require to live (or, if you're a company, the net profit plus your wages), this figure is probably reasonable. However, if the net profit doesn't cover your personal expenses, your business has a problem. (For more about budgeting for personal expenses, refer to Chapter 9.)

Thinking further ahead

In this chapter (and most other chapters in this book) I suggest you work on financial projections for the next 12-month period only. I make this suggestion for two reasons: First, if you're just getting started in business, trying to make financial projections for two, three or even five years into the future can quickly feel like a make-believe exercise, because so much about what lies ahead is unknown. Second, what I'm trying to do in this book is to get you to create financial projections yourself, and I don't want to discourage you by making things any trickier than they need to be.

However, if you only do financial projections for 12 months into the future, you may not get a true picture of what lies ahead, particularly if you have strong growth patterns or your business is just getting started. Sometimes, you need to extend your forecasts for 24 or even 36 months ahead in order to predict at what point your business will really start to flourish and generate decent profits.

Extending your Profit & Loss Projection is easy — simply copy and paste the results from the 12th month across to additional columns, and then change the figures as need be. All the same principles apply — you're simply extending the forecast for another year or two.

Taking Things a Step Further

A Profit & Loss Projection for the next 12 months provides a bare minimum for the financial part of your business plan. Other financial reports you may wish to include are a scenario analysis worksheet, a Cashflow Projection or a Balance Sheet Projection.

Measuring risk and your comfort factor

If you're doing a plan for a new business or a business that's currently undergoing significant change, one of the major challenges is how unknown everything is. For example, maybe you're planning to open up a new fashion outlet, a dentistry practice or a health spa. When it comes to forecasting your sales, you may feel that you're just plucking figures out of the air.

In this situation, I recommend you do a bit of scenario analysis, varying your income, cost of sales and expenses upwards or downwards by 10 or 20 per cent to see what happens. Although this process is slightly technical, it's probably the only way to assess how robust your plans are, and how much wriggle room you have to play with.

If you're new to Excel, I'll readily admit that scenario analysis can get a tad technical. For that reason, I provide a template that you can download and a short video that shows how to create a template of your own. To download the Building Scenarios worksheet or view the scenarios video, visit www.dummies. com/go/businessplanningessentials.

Looking at cashflow

Did you know that your business can make a profit yet can run out of cash? Of all the perils of business, one of the most disheartening has to be a promising enterprise that grows so fast that it starves itself of funds. However, if you have an eye to the future, not to mention the ability to create a Cashflow Projection report, you should be able to predict when a cash crunch is going to occur. You can then plan accordingly, maybe approaching the bank for additional finance, timing expenses differently or consciously slowing growth.

A Cashflow Projection is very similar to a Profit & Loss Projection, but with a few notable differences. I summarise these differences in Table 10-1.

Table 10-1	Differences between a Profit & Loss Projection and a Cashflow Projection
A Profit & Loss Projection . . .	*A Cashflow Projection . . .*
Shows sales in the month that they're made	Provides additional detail to show sales in the month that payment is received
Doesn't include incoming funds from loans or other sources of finance	Includes additional detail showing all sources of funds, including loans and capital contributions
Doesn't include consumer taxes (GST, VAT or sales tax) but shows all figures net of tax	More complex Cashflow Projections may show figures including tax, and then show tax payments separately
Shows only the interest on loan repayments, not the full value of the loan repayments	Shows the full value of loan repayments
Shows cost of sales (the cost of materials and so on) at the time a sale is made, regardless of when materials where purchased	Provides additional detail to show the purchase of materials in the month payment is made
Doesn't include capital expenditure or start-up costs	Includes all cash outflows, including capital expenditure and start-up costs
Doesn't include owner drawings	Includes a row to show owner drawings on projections for sole traders and partnerships
Includes no information regarding likely cash available	Calculates the closing bank balance for the end of each month

Is a Cashflow Projection an essential part of your business plan? If any of the following apply to your business, the answer is probably 'yes':

- ✔ If you offer credit to customers and your sales go up and down from month to month.

✔ If you hold inventory and inventory levels vary from month to month, or are likely to increase as your business grows.

✔ If you have major start-up costs or purchases of capital equipment that aren't shown in your Profit & Loss Projection.

✔ If your loan repayments are significantly different to interest expense (although an alternative approach is simply to show the full value of loan repayments in your Profit & Loss Projection).

The easiest way to create a Cashflow Projection is to download the Cashflow Projection worksheet from www.dummies. com/go/businessplanningessentials. This template shows you how the information flows from one bit of the Cashflow Projection to the next. You can also watch a video on the subject, accompanied by the dulcet, soothing tones of yours truly, also downloadable from www.dummies.com/go/ businessplanningessentials.

Creating Balance Sheet Projections

One of the reports that most business planning books suggest you include in the financial section of your plan is a Balance Sheet Projection. (Wondering what this is? A *Balance Sheet* is a report that provides a snapshot of your assets and liabilities at a single point in time. A *Balance Sheet Projection* is the same thing, but provides a forecast for some time in the future as to what you think your assets and liabilities will be.)

I'm hesitant about insisting on a Balance Sheet Projection as part of a business plan simply because this report requires a high level of accounting expertise. Unless you're using business-planning software, a Balance Sheet Projection will probably require that you get help from your accountant, which could be an additional expense you can ill afford.

You may think I'm not sounding very positive, but I like to think I'm a realist. In summary, if you're wondering whether to include a Balance Sheet Projection as part of your business plan, my answer is 'yes' if you have a method by which you can create this report quickly and easily (maybe you have a financial expert in-house or you're using business planning software). Otherwise, your time is probably better spent focusing on other tasks.

Chapter 11

Developing a Strong Marketing Plan

. . . .

In This Chapter

▶ Thinking about the structure of your marketing plan

▶ Looking at your customers, and the customers you want in the future

▶ Finetuning sales goals and strategies

▶ Incorporating a feedback loop to keep yourself honest

. . . .

*B*y its very nature, marketing is a creative process, usually driven more by impulse and instinct than by facts and figures. For this reason, I find that creating a structured marketing plan is every bit as important as creating a detailed financial plan.

In this chapter, I talk about the elements that make up a marketing plan, and walk you through important groundwork in regards to defining your target market and understanding who your customers really are. What is it that you're really selling and who do you want to sell this to? How do you set realistic sales targets and put strategies in place to make sure these targets are met? This chapter helps you work through these aspects.

With any marketing plan, you also need an element of review. Reviewing and measuring the results of your efforts provides the perfect counterweight for the sometimes intuitive nature of marketing, and enables you to be objective about what's working and what's not.

Laying Down the Elements

If you browse through a dozen business books you're likely to find that their formats for marketing plans all differ. Most of these formats have their merits, but here are the elements of a format I find works just fine:

- ✔ **Introduction:** Start with an engaging introduction that explains who you are, what you're selling, what kind of brand you're trying to build and your unique selling proposition. (I cover these topics in the next section.)

- ✔ **Target market:** Who are you selling to? Is your typical customer young or old, from the city or from the country? Later in this chapter, in 'Defining Your Target Market' I explain how to research this information.

- ✔ **Competitor analysis:** In this part of your marketing plan, you describe who your competitors are and how you compare. Chapter 3 focuses on competitor analysis, and in your marketing plan you almost certainly want to include a brief summary of this analysis.

- ✔ **Sales targets:** How much are you going to sell, who are you going to sell to and what is your pricing policy? See 'Setting Sales Goals and Strategies' for details.

- ✔ **Sales strategies:** What strategies do you intend to put in place to support your sales targets? Later in this chapter, 'Creating strategies to support your targets' outlines possible tactics.

- ✔ **Customer service:** A marketing plan isn't complete without an overview of how you plan to provide the best possible customer service. See 'Planning for Customer Service', later in this chapter, to find out more.

- ✔ **Review process:** The last section of this chapter, 'Keeping Yourself Honest', explains how to monitor your sales results, tweaking targets and strategies if necessary.

Writing an eloquent introduction

In Chapter 2 I suggest that you start your business plan with a strategic advantage statement that explains how your product or service benefits your customers and what differentiates your business from its competitors. As I explain in Chapter 2, this strategic advantage could be many things, including lower costs, a brilliant new idea, specialist skills, or the right to use certain intellectual property.

I reckon it works well if you start your marketing plan by reiterating this information — even if you choose to use different phrasing — so that you can reinforce what it is that you're trying to sell. Each business is different, but your strategic advantage usually forms the basis of the core messages that you need to convey to customers.

However, when you're selling this advantage to customers, and trying to encapsulate it in a few words, this advantage becomes your *USP* — your **U**nique **S**elling **P**oint.

If you're struggling to express your unique selling point in a few punchy words, I suggest you go online and search for businesses similar to your own. For example, maybe you offer a piano-tuning service. Search for similar businesses all around the world and check out their marketing slogans — 'We're in tune with you', 'Music to your ears', 'Stay sweet with the high notes'. I'm not suggesting you pinch someone else's selling point, but you can use it for inspiration.

The beauty of developing your own USP is that you can hone in on the thing that makes you different from your competitors, which is an infinitely better approach than trying to be all things to all people. Think about what you want your USP to be (or what it already is) and how you can best exploit this in your overall marketing.

Building a brand people want

I imagine that you have a pretty clear image of yourself and how you want the outside world to perceive you. You may see yourself as anything from a pearls and twin-set kind of gal to a double-income-no-kids executive, or from a freestyle hippy to a very straightforward farming bloke.

Your business needs an image just like you do. With a certain amount of forethought and awareness, you can build up this image. Businesses tend to have two types of image:

- ✔ The image of the business (sometimes also called *corporate branding*)

- ✔ The image of the things you sell (sometimes called *product branding*)

Think of your business as having its own identity, personality and image. This image is made up of lots of things, but includes the name and logo of your business, the quality of your products or services, and your displays and shop fittings. The appearance of your staff, the way in which you advertise, your colour schemes and the atmosphere that pervades your business premises all have a direct influence on the kind of image you present. When you're designing business cards, logos, signage or your website banners, don't do things on the cheap. Even if you have access to software that can do the job, keep in mind that it takes years of experience to develop an eye for design. Your brand is at stake every time you update your website, send an email with your logo at the bottom or create new advertising materials.

If you're still defining and building your brand, pause for a minute to consider how people will look for your product or services. If people are likely to look for you online, you want a company name (and brand) that includes words that say something about what you offer.

Defining Your Target Market

Traditionally, the second part of a marketing plan (the Introduction being the first part — refer to 'Writing an eloquent introduction', earlier in this chapter) is about defining your target market. For established businesses, defining your target market is largely about analysing who your current customers are; for businesses just getting started, defining your target market is about describing who you hope your customers are going to be.

Sometimes you may find that your customers end up being a different kind of customer than what you originally anticipated. You may be fine with this or you may decide that you want to change your mix of customers. In this situation, you need to implement specific sales targets and strategies to effect this change.

Try to use the following categories when painting this picture:

- ✔ **Demographics:** Is your typical customer male or female? How old are your customers and how much do they earn?

- ✔ **Geographic:** Where are your customers located? How many people live in this area? What's the climate?

✔ **Psychographic:** What kind of lifestyle does your typical customer aspire to? What motivates your customers?

✔ **Behavioural:** How often does a typical customer purchase from you? Are customers loyal to your business?

Go to www.dummies.com/go/businessplanningessentials to access a Customer Analysis template, which you can use as your starting point for customer analysis.

Thinking creatively about channels

In the next part of your marketing plan, devote some space to *channel analysis*. Sounds technical, but channel analysis is simply a description of each channel that you plan to sell through. Here are a few examples of channel analysis:

✔ **Nina has a retail store in the suburbs.** However, she also sells some clothes online. Her shop is one channel; eBay is another.

✔ **A manufacturer making gourmet jams sells through three different channels.** Direct to stores, in bulk to distributors and direct to consumers at farmers' markets.

✔ **Anita makes jewellery.** She sells some at the markets herself, some to a local gift store and some through a party plan. Each of these outlets is a channel.

✔ **An importer sells furniture via four different channels.** Large department stores, independent stores, online portals such as eBay and direct to customers from the warehouse shopfront.

Do you sell to more than one channel? (And if not, maybe you should!) If so, devote some of your marketing plan to describing each channel. Analyse what proportion of your sales goes to each channel and whether this channel is growing or declining.

Researching the market

If your business is very new or hasn't even started yet, I suggest you include some market research in your marketing plan. Market research sounds like such a technical term, but can be very simple in practice. Here are some examples:

✔ My son was thinking of starting a business working with local publishers selling book remainders on eBay. He tested his model by selecting one publisher and a small number of titles. (I could tell you the outcome of his research, but it's not such a happy tale.)

✔ Years ago, I had an idea to start up an online training company in partnership with a couple of other educational providers, specialising in QuickBooks software. As part of my market research, I looked carefully at companies providing similar services in different parts of the world. I discovered how none of these businesses seemed to be doing well and concluded that the market wasn't yet ready for this system of online training delivery.

✔ One of my girlfriends started a business selling gingham squares soaked in beeswax as an alternative to cling wrap. Part of her research process involved trialling different fabrics and sizes and giving samples to friends and family, asking for feedback about pricing and packaging.

Setting Sales Goals and Strategies

An essential part of any marketing plan is to set goals for sales and customer service. However, setting goals isn't enough — you also have to think about what strategies you're going to put in place to support these goals.

Thinking beyond the dollar

When you set sales targets for your business, avoid plucking random round figures out of the air; don't just plan to make sales of $20,000 every month, or sell 100 widgets in the next six months. Instead, break down your targets into bite-sized chunks, then apply a reality check to each one.

For example, a hairdresser could set targets as to the number of cuts and colours each week, a wholesaler might set targets for each geographic region (and sales rep) and an independent theatre could set targets for the number of tickets sold per day. (For more detail and templates to help you with this process, refer to Chapter 7.)

You may also like to set sales goals that aren't just expressed in dollars or units sold, but in other attributes as well. In Table 11-1, I list a few examples of sales goals that aren't measured in dollars. In the first column, I list long-term goals; in the second column, I list short-term goals; and in the third column, I list the strategies the business intends to employ in order to support these goals.

Table 11-1   Different Kinds of Sales Goals and How to Reach 'Em

Long-Term Aim	Sales Goal for the Quarter	Strategies to Support the Goal
Develop business in eastern suburbs	One new customer a week in this locality	Advertise in local online trading website
Improve booking rates from email queries	Make 10 bookings for every 25 queries	Set up templates for email replies
Increase repeat business	Repeat business to be 25% of total sales	Set up yearly reminders on database for all existing customers
Increase quality of service	Aim to reduce complaints to one a month	Further training for field staff and review of procedures
Improve on quote accuracy	Aim to ensure actual costs and time are within 10% of original quote	Issue weekly variance reports for each sales rep and meet every fortnight to discuss variances

Getting SMART

One of the acronyms consultants often employ when referring to goal setting is the SMART approach: A goal needs to be **S**pecific, **M**easurable, **A**chievable, **R**ealistic and **T**ime-specific.

I love the SMART approach and find it works really well. Here's the low-down on what each word means in practice:

- ✔ **Specific:** When talking about sales goals, are you being really precise about what you are hoping to achieve?
- ✔ **Measurable:** You need to able to measure every goal. (Dollars sold, units sold, new customers gained, email enquiries received, hits on the website and so on.)
- ✔ **Achievable:** Setting goals is pointless unless you can reasonably achieve them.

✔ **Realistic:** Even if a goal is potentially achievable, is it realistic? Do you definitely have enough time and enough funds to ensure the goal can be met?

✔ **Time specific:** Always specify the time frame for meeting this goal.

The sales goals outlined in Table 11-1 are pretty good in that they all seem to meet the SMART objectives (although, of course, it's hard for me to judge whether the goals in this example are definitely achievable and realistic).

Just for fun, here are some of the kinds of sales goals I really hate (they all sound cool at first glance, but scratch the surface and these goals are horrendously vague):

✔ 'I aim to increase online sales by 20 per cent.' (This goal fails the 'Time' test — by when will sales increase by this amount?)

✔ 'We plan to open a new store every six months for the next five years.' (Given that a new store costs about $80,000 to open, this goal almost certainly fails the 'Realistic' test.)

✔ 'My main goal is to improve customer satisfaction by 100 per cent.' (Unless you add a whole heap of detail, this goal fails the 'Measureable' test.)

✔ 'We will become a recognised brand.' (Yuck. I'm not even going to spell out all the tests this one fails.)

Creating strategies to support your targets

For every sales target you set, you want a marketing strategy that supports these targets. I like to organise strategies into four broad categories:

✔ Website and marketing materials

✔ Paid advertising (either online or in print)

✔ Public relations

✔ Networking (including social media)

Sounds easy, but what happens in practice is that people tend to gravitate towards marketing strategies that seem easy or appealing at the expense of strategies that are the most likely to succeed.

The instinct to stay in one's comfort zone can hold you back, big time. I regularly come across business owners who spend hundreds of hours mucking around with social media when what they really should be doing is knocking on doors and visiting people. Conversely, I also come across people spending too much money on print advertising instead of making the transition to online strategies.

Everyone has things they're good at and things they're bad at. However, your business doesn't want to know what you're good at; your business just wants what's good for it. With this in mind, here's my suggested plan of action:

1. **Read through the marketing strategies in this chapter (or any other business or marketing book for that matter).**

2. **Get together with your business partners or advisers and arrange a marketing meeting.**

   Of course, if the business is just you, take yourself out to a cafe or a quiet spot on a deserted headland. (Don't jump.)

3. **Brainstorm all the possible marketing ideas and write these down.**

   Remember the rules of brainstorming — even if someone comes up with an idea that's hopeless, or something that seems ridiculous pops into your head, you can't judge. Simply write down the idea and keep going.

4. **When the brainstorming process starts winding down, stop generating new ideas and instead highlight the 15 best ideas.**

   Ensure you have at least two ideas that relate to each of the four categories (websites/marketing materials, paid advertising, public relations and networking). If you don't, keep the ideas coming until you do.

5. **Next to the 15 best ideas, write approximate costs and the amount of time required. Score through any ideas that are plainly unaffordable.**

6. **Number these ideas from 1 to 15, with 1 being the idea you reckon will have most impact and 15 the least.**

At this point, don't worry about how much these ideas cost or how long they may take.

7. **Select the combination of ideas that you feel will give you most bang for your buck while falling within your total marketing budget. Then cross out any ideas that you know don't fit in your budget.**

   Make sure you continue to have a combination of ideas across the four categories. If you don't have a marketing budget yet, skip back to Chapter 9.

8. **With the amount of time you have available in mind, number your remaining ideas, starting with the number 1.**

   So idea 'number 1' will be within your marketing budget, achievable in a reasonable amount of time and guaranteed to generate sales. (If you still have more than 10 ideas on your list at this point, score through any ideas numbered 11 or higher.)

   You now have a list of marketing ideas, all within your budget and hopefully achievable in the time you have available, numbered 1 to 10 in order of priority.

9. **Set a schedule for each of the ideas on this list, then list which sales target each idea supports.**

   For more detail about this process, refer to 'Getting SMART' earlier in this chapter.

You may think that this process is a bit pedantic and, to be fair, it probably is. However, what this process safeguards you against is your own human nature. Your marketing priorities will be organised in a priority that hopefully fits the needs of your business, rather than what you're personally drawn to.

Planning for Customer Service

Ask successful businesspeople what they think their secret is, and chances are they say something about their customers. In fact, the majority of established businesses list customer service right at the top of attributes vital to their success.

Doing the right thing by your customers is the best possible form of advertising. The way you treat your customers influences their decision to come back to you; and because customers are getting more vocal about the value they place on being treated properly, listening reaps rewards. So, if something matters to customers, it has to matter to you too.

Customer service *does* mean different things to different people. I've heard excellent service described as 'being at your best with every customer' or 'figuring out new ways to help people'. Regardless of the description, the principle remains the same for all businesses — excellent service means always doing the right things, in the way customers want it done. Applying this principle in practice depends entirely on your business.

As part of your marketing plan, I suggest you include a few paragraphs summarising your customer service plan. In particular, you may want to include:

- Customer service goals (for example, your target response time for enquiries or order turnaround time)
- How you plan to get feedback from customers
- How your customer service standards compare with the competition
- How you intend to guarantee the consistency and quality of your products and/or services

Similar to your sales targets, your customer service goals should ideally be SMART (specific, measurable, achievable, realistic and time-specific — refer to the section 'Getting SMART', earlier in this chapter, for more).

To read more about planning for quality customer service, go to www.dummies.com/go/businessplanningessentials to download the Building a Customer Service Plan article.

Keeping Yourself Honest

The last part of your marketing plan is where you get to explain what systems you plan to put in place so that you track the effectiveness of your marketing campaigns.

Comparing targets and actuals

Early in this chapter I mention that a key attribute of any sales target is that it should be measurable (refer to the section 'Getting SMART'). For any sales targets that you express in dollars, one of the quickest ways to measure performance is to enter these targets as budgets in your accounting software. This way you can compare actuals versus budgets every month in a single click of a button, as I do in Figure 11-1.

July - June (Actuals vs. Budgets)	Actual	Budget	Difference
Income			
Sales Income			
Sales - Spring Water	$12,000.00	$10,000.00	$2,000.00
Sales - Carbonated Water	$5,201.00	$6,000.00	-$799.00
Sales - Water Cooler	$5,701.82	$20,000.00	-$14,298.18
Sales - Crock	$19,606.36	$20,000.00	-$393.64
Sales - Stands	$21,468.19	$5,000.00	$16,468.19
Sales - Other Equip	$9,272.72	$2,000.00	$7,272.72
Freight	$899.00	$1,500.00	-$601.00
Service Income			
Service - Coolers	$29,600.00	$30,000.00	-$400.00
Service - Other Income	$21,290.91	$22,000.00	-$709.09
Time Billing Income			
Consultancy Income	$8,200.00	$7,000.00	$1,200.00
Travelling Time	$17,456.37	$15,000.00	$2,456.37
Secretarial Income	$181.81	$500.00	-$318.19
Km Travelled	$1,818.19	$2,000.00	-$181.81
Photocopying Income	$109.09	$200.00	-$90.91
Currency Gain Loss	$0.00	$0.00	$0.00
Income	$152,805.46	$141,200.00	$11,605.46
Cost Of Sales			

Help F1 · Print · Filters · Up · Down · Dollar · Percent · Sales · Net P&L · Close

Figure 11-1: Try to compare actual sales results against budgets on a regular basis.

The downside about simply comparing actual results against budgeted targets is that you can only evaluate the overall success of your sales targets, and you don't get to see the detail that lies behind. For example, your total sales might be close to the combined total of your sales targets, but if you analyse the whole deal more closely, you could find that actual sales via your website exceeded targeted sales by 20 per cent, but actual sales made via the weekend markets fell short by about the same amount.

Tracking referral sources

You probably know the advertising maxim: 'You know that only one dollar of every hundred dollars you spend on advertising works. The thing you don't know is which dollar it is.' However, while this saying is chillingly true, you can still build up an idea of how effective your advertising strategies are with strategies such as the following:

- ✔ **Keep track of loyalty schemes:** If you offer discounts or loyalty schemes, record these discounts separately in your point-of-sale system (or cash register), or in a separate income category in your accounting software. This way you can keep track of how much you give out in discounts and, therefore, how well this type of advertising works.

- ✔ **Publish unique contact details:** If you want to test a new form of advertising, try publishing a unique phone number (a VOIP number is usually cheapest), email address or website landing page, so that you can readily identify all leads generated by the ad.

- ✔ **Record referral sources:** The easiest way to collect this data is when someone first makes contact, asking how this potential customer heard about your business. Record the response in your database and/or accounting software. Later, when you generate sales reports, correlate how many sales were made as a result of each source.

Analysing online success

When analysing the effectiveness of online advertising, remember that the purpose of this form of advertising isn't just to create sales. Online advertising forms a part of your overall marketing strategy, one part of which is almost certainly to build customer awareness of your products and services. Don't get too hooked on measuring online advertising in dollars and cents — even if visitors didn't buy a product or make an enquiry today, they may return to your website in the future. With this in mind, here are some of the performance measures you can use for online advertising:

- ✔ **Analyse ranking on key search engines for keywords:** I don't really have scope here to talk in detail about keywords, but suppose that your business is holiday accommodation on the north coast. In this scenario 'holiday accommodation north coast' is certainly a keyword, and you can measure how you rank on this keyword by typing the phrase into Google (or any other search engine) to see where your website appears. For example, if you're the sixth entry on the second page, and each page has 10 entries, you rank 16th for this keyword.

Make a list of all keywords for your website and track your ranking for each of these keywords once a month. Monitor how your performance changes each month.

✔ **Analyse website traffic:** Subscribe to a website traffic analysis tool (Google Analytics is one of the best and it's free) so that you can monitor how people find your website, what web pages they visit, and how long people stay after they get there. Correlate changes in traffic with any new marketing strategies you put in place, so that you can accurately measure the effect of these strategies.

✔ **Set up conversion tracking on paid online advertising:** Try to define what you want visitors to do as a result of browsing your website or Facebook page. Maybe you want them to make an enquiry, subscribe to your newsletter, buy a product from your online store, view session times, make an appointment or sign up to a forum board. In web-nerd lingo, each of these outcomes is called a conversion. Depending what web stats program you're using, you can add little bits of HTML code (the mark-up language used to publish web pages) that track every conversion made, and whether this conversion originated from paid online advertising or not.

Chapter 12

Pulling Together Your Written Plan

. . . .

In This Chapter

▶ Examining the skeleton of your plan — a quick anatomy lesson

▶ Creating a concise summary of who you are and where you're at

▶ Assembling key financial documents

▶ Keeping yourself on track — a schedule for each turn on the road

. . . .

*I*f you've been working on your plan over the course of the last few days or even weeks, you may be feeling that your brain is turning to mush. You may have ended up with a random pile of notes, a folder of partially written Word documents, and a ragtag assembly of financial projections and reports.

Don't worry. In this chapter, I show you how the pieces of the business-plan jigsaw fit together. This stage is undoubtedly the most exciting of the whole planning process. You get to take a step back, see how everything interconnects and experience that warm glow of self-belief as you think, 'Yes, I can succeed and this plan explains just how.'

In this chapter, I also share heaps of tips for keeping things real. Business plans too quickly slip into buzzwords and woolly promises. I reflect on the relative merits of mission statements and emphasise the importance of financials, sales targets and clear marketing plans.

With an eye on the future, I also explain how to translate your big-picture goals into bite-sized chunks that you can plan to achieve next month, next week or right this very moment.

Reviewing the Overall Structure

You can organise your business plan in any way you like, but a format that works well (and which reflects how I've organised the chapters in this book) is as follows:

- ✔ **Cover page and table of contents.** Your final business plan will probably end up being between 15 and 20 pages long, so a table of contents helps others find what's what.

- ✔ **Business overview, company description (including your strategic advantage), and a summary of key goals.** To find out more, see 'Introducing Your Business' next in this chapter.

- ✔ **A competitor analysis, industry analysis and SWOT analysis.** Refer to Chapters 3 and 4 for information on how to structure this information.

- ✔ **Financial reports, including Profit & Loss Projections (essential) and Profit & Loss historical reports (essential unless you're a brand new business).** Other optional reports include break-even analysis, Cashflow Projections, ratio analysis, Balance Sheet reports and budgets. See 'Plunging into the Financials', later in this chapter, for more details.

- ✔ **A people plan and a summary of operations.** In this part you summarise your skills and the skills of others involved in your business. Depending on your business type, you may also include a summary of operations. See 'Selling yourself and your team' and 'Providing a quick summary of operations' later in this chapter.

- ✔ **Your marketing plan.** Chapter 11 provides a complete summary of how to construct a marketing plan.

- ✔ **A risk-management plan.** A risk-management plan needs to explain how you intend to protect your intellectual property, guard against litigation and what insurance coverage you intend to have.

- ✔ **A summary of goals and an action plan, along with any appendices or extra information.** See 'Setting Milestones for Every Step of the Way', in this chapter.

Please don't feel obliged to stick to my suggested structure. In particular, if you've chosen to use business-planning software (a topic I cover in Chapter 1), you'll almost certainly end up with a structure that's slightly different. I reckon the sequence of information is irrelevant, so long as you end up covering the topics I list in the checklist in Table 12-1.

Table 12-1 **Your Business Plan Checklist**

Planning Item	Essential or Optional?
OVERALL SUMMARY	
Non-disclosure agreement	Include if your plan contains confidential information
An inspirational description of your company and what it does	Essential
A mission statement	Optional, but an expected part of a standard business plan
A values statement	Only include if you truly intend to commit to these values
A clear statement of how your business is different and a summary of strategic advantage	Essential
A summary of the major goal or goals for your business for the next 12 to 24 months	Essential
FINANCIALS	
Detailed sales budgets for the next 12 months, along with a summary of how you arrived at these budgets	Essential
If you've been trading for more than a year, a Profit & Loss for the last 12 months	Essential
If you've been trading for more than a year, a Balance Sheet generated for the last day of your Profit & Loss reporting period	Essential
A Profit & Loss Projection for at least 12 months ahead	Essential
A Cashflow Projection	Essential if you're predicting growth and you carry stock or offer credit to customers

(continued)

Table 12-1 *(continued)*

Planning Item	Essential or Optional?
A budget for the next 12 months (your Profit & Loss Projection may be able to double as a budget)	Essential
Moving annual turnover analysis	Useful for seasonal businesses
Detailed product costings	Essential for manufacturers
MARKETING	
An analysis of who your customers currently are, and (if different) who you want them to be in the future	Essential
A detailed competitor analysis	Essential
A summary of the sales strategies you have in place, or intend to have in place, to support your sales targets	Essential
A customer service plan	Essential
PEOPLE	
A description of the skills and experience of both yourself and the others in your team	Essential
STRATEGIC	
A summary of operations (distribution methods, premises, manufacturing processes and so on)	Often not relevant for service businesses
An analysis of the industry in which you belong, the trends in this industry, and how you intend to be responsive to change	Essential
A summary (and action plan) of strengths, weaknesses, opportunities and threats	Essential
A risk-management plan	Essential
ACTION	
A summary of goals and objectives	Essential
An action plan summarising the timeframe for achieving these goals and objectives	Essential

Go to www.dummies.com/go/businessplanningessentials to download a copy of the Business Plan Checklist in Table 12-1, which includes a column where you can tick off each item as you complete it.

Introducing Your Business

Most business plans start with a summary that includes a mission statement, a brief company description and a summary of overall strategy (including a description of what makes this business different from other similar businesses). Many plans also include a values statement.

Devising a mission statement

Now for something a little radical: I'm not sure I really believe in mission statements. (Wondering what I'm talking about? A *mission statement* is a simple sentence or couple of sentences describing what your business is about.) Unless such a statement is superbly crafted with great insight, I reckon mission statements are about as useful as an umbrella in a bushfire.

Despite this general cynicism, if you intend to share your plan with others, a mission statement will be expected. So what's involved?

- ✓ **Keep your statement short and sweet.** Don't be tempted to write too much — if your mission statement is more than two sentences long, or it can't fit into the standard Twitter 140-character template, ditch it and begin again.

- ✓ **Make your statement inspirational.** 'My mission is to earn lots of money and retire by the time I'm 40' just isn't going to cut it, especially in the eyes of employees or customers. Try to create a mission with the potential to inspire and motivate others.

- ✓ **Reserve jargon for public servants.** For a humorous read on this topic, I recommend *Death Sentence: The Decay of Public Language* by Don Watson and published by Random House.

- ✓ **Look for inspiration online.** No-one but you can come up with an authentic mission statement, but if you run short on ideas, try checking out the missions of other businesses similar to your own. Go to a search engine like Google and type the words **mission statement** plus a word to cover whatever line of business you're in (for example, type: mission statement plumbing company).

✔ **Don't just cobble a few words together.** A good mission statement is no substitute for a bad business plan. Your customers aren't idiots and generally have a sniffer-dog instinct for drivel.

Some companies talk about creating *vision statements* as well as mission statements. In this context, a vision statement encapsulates long-term goals and aspirations, along with the ideals that a business is striving for, whereas a mission statement is more about stating what you do, why you do it and whom for. I find that the boundaries between these two kinds of statements get blurred, and for most situations, believe that a simple mission statement does just fine.

By the way, after you create your mission statement, don't forget to update your website or any other key marketing materials with what you state in your mission statement.

Crafting a company description

Imagine that someone who has never met you or traded with you before is reading your plan. How would you describe your business so that this person gets a good sense of who you are and what you do? With this scenario in mind, start writing, aiming for three of four paragraphs in total and keeping the following in mind:

Your strategic advantage and what differentiates you from your competitors. This point is the single most important thing to include on the first page of your plan. For more on this topic, refer to Chapter 2.

✔ **How long your business has been running.** If your business has been running for some considerable time, say so. Be proud of your accomplishment.

✔ **The turnover of your business and the number of employees.**

✔ **The kind of services your business provides.** Be specific. If you're a physiotherapist, say what your area of speciality is and who your customers are.

✔ **The kind of industry your business belongs to.** Talk about your particular industry, what the trends are and what factors are peculiar to it.

✔ **Your main goal or goals.** If your goal is to reach sales of 10,000 units within two years, say so.

✔ **The scope of opportunity.** Flesh out the full extent of any possible opportunities, particularly if your plan is going to be read by a possible investor.

Refining your overall strategy

In Chapters 3 and 4, I talk about analysing your competitors in the context of what's going on in the industry and what you do best. These topics are broad, so how do you decide what information to include in your plan? Consider the following:

✔ **An analysis of your industry:** Try to include at least one to two paragraphs on each of the following topics (unless a particular topic is irrelevant to your industry): the potential impact on your business of any changes in competitor activity, environmental factors, exchange rates, outsourcing patterns from overseas, government legislation or technology. The analysis should also include a general overview of overall trends in pricing and the growth or decline of the industry as a whole.

With this analysis, if you have sourced expert reports regarding industry trends, summarise the gist of these reports in one or two sentences in the main body of your plan, but consider including the full report at the end of your plan as an appendix.

✔ **Your SWOT analysis:** I explain how to do a SWOT analysis in Chapter 4. It's up to you whether you only include the final 'SWOT grid' or you choose to include the workings that lie behind this grid, including the detailed analysis of your strengths and weaknesses. I generally feel that the more information you include in this part of your plan, the better.

✔ **A risk-management plan:** Ensure that you adequately cover the topics of protecting intellectual property and insurance. (Any lender or outside investor is going to want reassurance that you have these areas covered.)

You can find a neat template for a risk-management plan at
www.dummies.com/go/businessplanningessentials.

Plunging into the Financials

In working on the financial part of your plan, you may well have
ended up with a wide selection of documents — everything from
product costings to price comparisons, from historical sales
reports to budgets for the years ahead. Which reports should
you include in your final plan, and in what sequence should you
present these?

Presenting your key reports

Here's a summary of the key financial reports you should
consider including in your plan:

- If your business is new, include a summary of start-up
  expenses and how you plan to finance these.

- Always include a Profit & Loss Projection for at least the
  next 12 months. If your business is growing quickly, extend
  this projection and include figures for the next 24 to 36
  months as well. (For subsequent years, you can summarise
  projections to include one column per quarter, rather than
  one column per month.)

- If your business has been trading a while, include a
  historical Profit & Loss for the last 12 months. Hopefully
  you use accounting software, so you can generate this
  report easily. If you don't, you may need to supply the
  Profit & Loss report from your most recent tax return. If the
  figures for the past 12 months are unusual for any reason,
  include some notes as to why.

- Similarly, if your business has been trading a while, include
  a Balance Sheet right up to the end of the period that your
  Profit & Loss spans — if your Profit & Loss report goes
  from April to March, generate a Balance Sheet for 31 March.
  Again, if you use accounting software, you can generate a
  Balance Sheet in a flash.

- If your business teeters on the edge of profitability or
  fails to generate enough profit for you to live comfortably,
  break-even analysis can be very helpful. (For more
  information on how to calculate break-even analysis, see

Creating a Business Plan For Dummies, also written by me and published by Wiley.)

- ✔ A Cashflow Projection report can be technical and time-consuming to create. However, you only really need this report if you're predicting growth for your business *and* you offer credit to customers or carry a significant amount of inventory.

- ✔ A Balance Sheet Projection predicts the value of assets, liabilities and equity at the end of the period that your Profit & Loss Projection spans. (So if your Profit & Loss Projection goes from April 2014 to March 2015, your Balance Sheet Projection forecasts account balances for 31 March 2015.) Unless you use business planning software, creating your own Balance Sheet Projections is normally out of reach for most ordinary mortals, and a Cashflow Projection is (mostly) a valid substitute.

- ✔ Depending on your business, you may want to provide more detail for some expense items in your Profit & Loss Projection, so that you can set down clear budgets for the year ahead. For example, you may want to grab the total figure for Advertising Expense and split this into a detailed budget for different marketing activities.

 When you create financial projections, you have to make many assumptions along the way. Maybe you've assumed that you're going to hire a new employee in three months' time, shift premises, or that a new sales contract is going to come through. Even if the plan is for your eyes only, include these assumptions in your narrative.

You may even want to include multiple scenarios in this part of your plan: What if sales were 10 per cent higher or expenses 20 per cent lower?

Pleading for finance

If one of the purposes of your plan is to apply for a loan or hustle for investor funds, you want to include a coherent plea for finance in your plan. This plea should include how much finance you require and when, how long you want to borrow this money for, the interest you expect to pay and your proposed repayment schedule.

Be ultra-careful to ensure your financial projections reflect the need for finance and the proposed repayment plan. Your Cashflow Projection is ideal for corroborating the need for additional finance, because this report predicts your cash balance at the end of each month and quickly highlights predicted cash shortfalls.

Don't forget to include the anticipated loan interest as an expense in your Profit & Loss Projection, and also include the full value of proposed loan repayments in your Cashflow Projection. Alternatively, if your plan doesn't include a Cashflow Projection, show the full value of the loan repayment in the Profit & Loss Projection.

Completing the Rest of Your Plan

The last ten or so pages of your plan include your people plan, a summary of operations, your marketing plan, SWOT analysis and risk-management plan. When collating this information, keep returning in your mind to your overall goals and business strategy. How well do the pieces fit together?

Look for consistency. If your marketing plan budgets for a significant growth in sales, is this growth reflected in your people plan (in other words, do you intend to recruit more staff)? If your SWOT analysis shows a weakness in working with social media, does the Facebook strategy that forms the keystone of your marketing plan make sense?

Selling yourself and your team

One of the things I try to convey to people just getting started in business is that you must think of your business as being separate from yourself. In order to grow, you need to involve others so that you can leverage your business idea and expertise. This need to conceive of your business as a separate entity in its own right is why the people part of your plan is so important. (I explore this topic in some depth in Chapter 5.)

For the purposes of your plan, all you need to do is write a concise description about the key people involved in the business and who is responsible for doing what. If you're only

just getting started — maybe you don't have any employees
yet — include details of people in your network who are
assisting you, such as your accountant, business mentor,
family or friends. Write a short description of each person's
role, including relevant work experience and qualifications,
and don't hesitate to emphasise the unique skills each person
contributes. (I don't normally suggest you include résumés or
CVs in a business plan, but if you feel such a document would be
relevant, stick it in your plan's appendixes.)

If you've identified any particular weaknesses within your
company — maybe you're not strong on financials or you don't
have anybody in your business who's confident with social
media — consider addressing this weakness in your people plan
and explain how you intend to manage this.

Providing a quick summary of operations

I don't really dwell much on operations elsewhere in this book,
but if you're a manufacturer or wholesaler, I suggest you include
a brief summary of operations management at this point in
your plan. This summary typically describes the process of
manufacture, where and how your product is manufactured, and
what mechanisms you have in place for order fulfilment and
delivery.

What to include in this part of a plan is very specific to each
business. Maybe you're tossing up whether to manufacture
in-house or to outsource production; maybe supply and demand
are difficult to manage and you have long lead times when
ordering materials. Order fulfilment can also be tricky: Do you
plan to distribute goods yourself? How will you manage freight?
Are the costs of order fulfilment so high that you need to get a
certain level of orders before you break even?

The name of the game with most manufacturing and wholesale
businesses is profit margins, where a change of 1 or 2 per
cent can spell the difference between success and failure. The
operations side of things (warehouse rent, staff, freight, order
processing and so on) is often where a significant chunk of profit
gets chewed up, especially for growing businesses where staff
requirements change frequently.

Introducing the killer marketing plan

In Chapter 11, I run through the key elements of a marketing plan: The introduction, a target market analysis, a competitor analysis, a summary of sales targets, a summary of sales strategies and a customer service plan.

The main thing when working on the marketing section of a business plan is to ensure that the figures in your marketing plan correlate dollar for dollar with the figures in your financials. So if your predicted sales for the next 12 months in your marketing plan are $252,000, ensure your Profit & Loss Projection says exactly the same thing.

Setting Milestones for Every Step

As you progress through your plan, you inevitably end up with a list of goals, including financial goals, sales goals, customer conversion goals, personal goals and product goals. Some of these goals may reflect that you still have extra distance to go with the planning process, or some may reflect the necessity to keep reviewing your plan every six months or so.

In the last part of your plan, I suggest you bring all of these goals together into a single schedule and create the planning calendar from hell. Start by reading through every line of your business plan and thinking about what action you need to take. For example, maybe in your SWOT analysis you identified a weakness in that you haven't yet trademarked your logo and business name. Translate this weakness into a plan of action — decide when you want to initiate trademark application procedures, and set a time frame.

When creating an action plan, you may want to try to differentiate between *goals* and *objectives*. Goals are the overarching aim of the game; objectives are the means by which you get there. Table 12-2 gives you an idea of how to make this distinction.

If you don't want to bother with the semantics of separating goals and objectives, that's fine too. The main thing is to remember that the best goals are always SMART: **S**pecific, **M**easurable, **A**chievable, **R**ealistic and **T**ime-specific. (I explain this terminology in Chapter 11, but the words give you some idea of what's required.)

Table 12-2	Creating an Action Plan	
Goal	*Objective*	*Time Frame*
Stay aware of changes in competitors	Review competitor analysis	Six-monthly
	Visit at least five competitor shops and report back	March
Stay within 5% of budgets for the next 12 months	Enter monthly budgets into accounting software	Annual
	Compare actuals against budgets in Profit & Loss	Monthly
Get on top of bookkeeping and produce accurate financial reports	Hire a bookkeeper ASAP and ensure accounts are reconciled weekly	Weekly check
Increase gross profit margin by 5% within 6 months	Research ways to reduce product costs, particularly packaging	Ongoing
	Look at changing freight companies to reduce shipping	Ongoing
Meet or exceed sales targets for the next 12 months	Sign up one new customer every week	Weekly
	Aim to find one new distributor to serve western seaboard	By October
	Update email templates	Now
	Sign up for Google Adwords (budget equals $40 per week)	Do now, review monthly
	Report actuals against marketing budget every month	Monthly

(continued)

Table 12-2 *(continued)*

Goal	Objective	Time Frame
Protect intellectual property and brand	Get help to create formal employee agreements and include a non-disclosure agreement as part of same	October
	Commence trademark application	September
Stay abreast of industry trends	Attend monthly industry association meetings	Monthly
	Review industry statistics	Six-monthly
Secure business against potential litigation	Draw up a product recall policy	February
	Review all insurance policies	Annual

After you clarify your planning goals, along with the time frame and frequency for each goal, transfer these goals onto a business-planning calendar for the next 12 months.

Depending on the size of your business, you may even decide to create several business planning calendars according to who is responsible for what. However, as the owner, you still want to keep an eye on everyone's planning calendar, not just your own, so that you can be sure nothing falls by the wayside.

Chapter 13

Ten (Almost!) Questions to Ask before You're Done

In This Chapter

▶ Doctoring the spin in 30 seconds or less

▶ Facing up to your competition

▶ Making sure the numbers are right

▶ Imagining a future beyond this business

Do you feel you've created a business plan that's as good as can be for the time being? Great! Before you sign off, check your plan one last time, asking yourself the quick questions contained in this chapter.

Can You Summarise Your Business in 30 Seconds or Less?

When I was mentoring start-up businesses at a local business college, I would always begin the very first session by asking students to summarise their business in 30 seconds or less—an 'elevator speech'. Each student had to include both a description of their business and state what made their business special. I was strict about the time limit, holding a stopwatch and calling out 'STOP' as soon as 30 seconds ticked around.

At that first session, I'd usually find that only one or two students could jump this hurdle. So I would persist, starting at least one session every week (the course ran for eight weeks) by repeating the exercise. As everyone's business plans progressed, more and more students were able to articulate the essential purpose of their business, and why they felt their business had potential.

How do you rate at this exercise? Try this:

1. **Ready? Lay your hands on a recording device.**

   Your smartphone or the Sound Recorder application on your computer will do the job.

2. **Set? Find a timepiece.**

   Does anybody still have a watch? I know I don't. But I do have a great big red clock in my kitchen with the noisiest most infuriating tick in the world.

3. **Go! Click Record and talk aloud, describing your business and what's so special about it.**

   Don't talk for more than 30 seconds and if you stuff up your speech the first time, try again straightaway.

How did you go? When you listen to yourself, do you feel impressed by your succinct expression and winning communication style? Hopefully! But if not, take heart. First, head back to Chapter 2 to read about identifying strategic advantage for your business.

After working on your 30-second summary, read through the introductory section of your business plan one more time. If you can't articulate the essence of your business at the drop of a hat, chances are the introduction to your plan may be a little weak. Read through these pages and rework if necessary.

Does Your Plan Truly Evaluate Competitors?

One thing I've observed when looking at business plans, particularly plans for new businesses, is how many people gloss over competitor analysis. I find this a real worry, because understanding competitors is so essential to doing well in business.

I think I've figured out the psychology of this head-in-the-sand behaviour. When businesses are new, the 'dream' is still relatively intact. Spending too much time looking at competitors can make you feel like this dream is getting crushed, and in place of hope you may get a sense of anxiety about going head-to-head with the big guys in town.

Don't worry. Although competition is always a little scary, it can be inspirational too. By analysing your competitors in depth, you may find ideas that you want to imitate, ways you can adapt your pricing to increase profits, or new market niches that you hadn't been aware of.

So remember, if you haven't analysed competitors properly, your plan isn't complete. (If you're wondering what form a proper analysis takes, skip back to Chapter 3.)

Have You Double-Checked Your Numbers?

I spend a fair chunk of this book discouraging you from adding up figures using a calculator and instead advocating the use of a spreadsheet. Now I'm going to eat my hat. Before you finalise your plan, grab a copy of every financial report you've created using a spreadsheet and add up at least one column using a calculator.

Have I gone bananas? Not really. Spreadsheets provide an excellent way to create financial projections, but they can be prone to error. For example, if you insert a sum at the bottom of a column of figures and then later you insert an additional row just above this sum, the formula may not always update automatically. You may end up with a total at the bottom of a long column of figures that misses the last number, thereby misleading you and everyone else.

As well as the automatic summing in Excel, while you're at it check other logic too. For example, if your sales projections involve multiplying units sold by a particular unit price, manually check at least one or two months of sales projections to ensure the totals are correct.

Do Your Numbers Fit Your Goals?

In Chapter 12, I talk about setting goals and objectives for every element in your plan, along with a time frame for each one. As one final check, evaluate how much each one of these objectives is going to cost (in both time and money), and then return to your Profit & Loss Projection to see if the numbers match up.

For example, if one of your goals is to launch a Google Adwords campaign next March, does your budget for Advertising Expense increase in March accordingly? Or if one of your goals is to open a new retail outlet in November, does your Profit & Loss Projection show a corresponding increase in Rental Expense and Wages Expense from that month onwards?

In addition, if any goals involve a time commitment from you, pause to consider whether this time involves any additional costs. For example, maybe one of your goals is to call on at least three new stores per week from February onwards. If the person calling on those stores is you, do you have enough time? If your intention is to do this task but maybe flick-pass something else you currently do to an employee, have you budgeted enough in Wages Expense?

Have You Cast Your Net as Wide as Possible?

I love this part of the review process. Here's what you need:

- ✔ **A kid-free zone.** Things are looking up.
- ✔ **At least two hours free time.** Hard to find, easy to lose.
- ✔ **No TV, internet or mobile phone.** Can't bring yourself to switch off? Drive to a place with no signal.
- ✔ **A couple of sheets of A3 paper and coloured pens.** I'm sounding really old school but believe me, this method works.

Now with your feet up and your mind free from distractions, let yourself dream. How big could your business be? What avenues have you yet to explore? Who could you partner with? Do you have any crazy ideas that just won't go away?

Give these ideas some room to bloom, and see where the journey takes you. Then return to your business plan and see whether these fresh insights can help you to boost the visionary element of your plan.

Have You Made Any Assumptions You Can't Justify?

Almost any business plan includes some assumptions. Maybe you've assumed that sales will grow at a certain rate, your lease will be renewed or that you're going to upgrade your equipment. Or, if you're planning for a new business, maybe you've made assumptions about the size of the market, what price points customers are going to find acceptable, or the rate of repeat business.

For every assumption that you make in your plan, try first to spell out the assumption, then second, provide the rationale. Here are some examples:

- A plan assumes certain product costs, then provides detailed costing sheets in the appendix to justify these.

- A plan shows sales growth of 5 per cent per year, then explains this by graphing last year's sales and showing this as a trend.

- A plan shows sales growth of 20 per cent, but includes wages for a new sales agent in the budget.

- A plan shows a move away from bricks-and-mortar retail towards online sales, then justifies this by including an industry report that indicates this trend.

 Industry-specific analysis is like gold for a business plan. If you can get hold of a good industry report, especially one analysing long-term trends, refer to this report in your plan and possibly include this report in the appendix.

Similarly, try to demonstrate a sophisticated, in-depth understanding of who your customers are, including who buys from you and why, and in what quantities.

What Do Others Think?

Once you reckon you've done as much as you can on your business plan, start sharing your plan with others. Show the financial section of your plan to your accountant, share your plan with family or friends. If you have employees, ask them to look through the plan and provide feedback.

Next, seek professional feedback from a business adviser or mentor. If you can't afford a consultant, that's fine. Many government advisory centres offer free business advice, and will be happy to review your plan.

And remember, your business plan isn't a literary work. Not just because your plan doesn't include mystery murders, engaging dialogue and risqué sex scenes — more's the pity — but also because, unlike a novel, your business plan is never finished. Be open to feedback and comments, and be prepared to let your plan continually evolve.

Do You Have a Get-Out Plan?

Do you have a plan for selling your business? You may be bemused by this question, especially if you haven't actually started your business yet and you're still at the planning stage. However, if you're able to conceive of a future for your business that's independent of you and that you can sell to someone else, you've made the leap in thinking from being a businessperson to being an entrepreneur.

Is Your Plan Inspirational?

I'm not a true risk taker, which is probably one of the reasons I find business planning a comforting activity. Much of the business plan process focuses on being *sensible*: Checking financials, looking at margins, evaluating risk and so on.

Yet often it's the wackiest business ideas that work. Who would have thought that Crocs, those ugly spa shoes made from brightly coloured resin, could become an international fashion item? Or that the Pet Rock would be a fad that swept the world? (The Pet Rock was nothing more than a plain grey pebble packaged in a small box accompanied by a tongue-in-cheek Pet Rock training manual. With a statistic that does nothing to credit human intelligence, entrepreneur Gary Dahl sold over 5 million units in less than six months.)

Balance figures with fun, caution with creativity and budgets with belief. Let daring and hope be the spark that energises your business plan, and endeavour to infect yourself, your plan and others with an overriding sense of optimism.

Index

• A •

action plans, 48, 158–160
analysing
  customers, 136–137
  net profit, 127
  success, 59
annual expenses, budgeting for, 113
Apple, 23, 79
applying for finance, 155
assets
  management strategies, 72, 73
  owned personally, 69
  versus expenses, 67
assumptions, justifying, 155, 165
AutoSum (Excel), 110

• B •

Balance Sheets, 131, 154
Balance Sheet Projections, 131, 155
behavioural analysis, 137
benchmarking
  as a way of reducing risk, 129
  Profit & Loss Projections, 154
  sales targets, 138
billable hours, calculating, 84–85
bookkeeping equation, 131
borrowing, 75. *See also* finance, loans
  from family
brainstorming, 141
branding, 61, 136
break-even analysis, 154
budgeting
  comparing against actuals, 14, 143
  for expenses, 107–118
  for marketing, 142, 158
  for start-up, 65–75

building systems, 60
building scenarios, 129
business advisory centres, 9, 166
business angels, 74
business expense templates, 109,
  112–113
business leases, 73
business loans, 73
business models. *See also* strategic
  advantage
  assessing, 119, 127
  cost-based pricing, 78
  scoring, 16–18
  sparking inspiration, 164, 166
business performance quiz,
  40–41
business plans
  calendar for action, 160
  checklist, 149–151, 161
  different formats, 8
  elements of, 11
  getting help with, 9
  how much time required, 7
  how often to update, 15
  length of, 7
  long-term vision, 49–55
  period for plan, 107
  software, 9
  structure of, 11, 147
  templates, 9
  when to start, 8
  who they are for, 8
business planning courses, 9
business planning cycle, 15
business planning software, 10,
  11, 131
Business Plans Pro, 10
business scorecard, 16–18
buzzwords, 166

• C •

calculating billable hours
  worksheet, 85
calendars (for planning), 158–160
capital expenditure, 130
cash versus profit, 130
Cashflow Projections, 14,
  129–131, 155
cells (Excel), naming, 105
change, planning for, 48, 158
channel analysis, 137
checking your business idea, 3
checklists
  business plan elements, 151
  identifying variable costs, 93
  importance of, 60
  online, 3
  Profit & Loss Projection, 126
  topics to include in your plan, 149
cloud-based software, 10
collateral (for loans), 72, 74
comfort zone, avoiding, 141
commissions, 93
company description, 151, 152
company tax, 116, 125
competitive advantage. *See also*
    strategic advantage
  summarising, 161
  understanding, 19–20, 32–35
competitor analysis
  checking, 162
  future competitors, 35–36
  importance of, 28–29
  industry trends, 35
  profiling, 29
  summarising, 138
  where to include in your plan,
    134, 150
  worksheet, 30–32
competitor-based pricing, 78, 80
competitors
  differentiating yourself from, 135
  entry barriers, 35
  future, 35

head-to-head, 31–32
new, 42
online, 36
rating, 33
threats, 36
complaints, procedures for, 61
consistency, 60
constraints to growth, 63
contractors. *See* subcontract
  labour
conversion tracking, 146
corporate branding, 135
cost leadership strategy, 33
cost of goods sold, 67, 92–97
cost-based pricing, 78, 80
costs. *See also* expenses
  calculating, 92–97
  incoming, 95
  manufacturers, 96
  outgoing, 95
  product costings, 104
  reducing, 72
  services provided, 94
  valuing labour, 97
  varying exchange rates, 95
  when importing, 95
  worksheets, 95
creative business, limitations of, 63
credit cards, 73
custom manufacture, 97
customers
  analysing growth, 36
  defining your market, 136
  getting feedback from, 138, 143
  profiling needs, 136
  purchase frequency, 136
  template for analysis, 137
customer service, 61, 134, 142

• D •

debt finance, 73–74
demand, being realistic about, 89
demographic analysis, 136
demographic change, 43

difference, defining yours, 58
differential pricing, 81, 83
differentiation strategy, 33–34
direct costs, 92
discounts, 83, 96
distribution
  costing imports, 95
  entry barriers, 35
  start-up stock requirements, 66
  summarising in your plan, 150
dreams, realising, 17, 126
dummies.com, 3

• E •

eco-opportunties, 44
economy, analysing change in, 43
elevator speech, 24, 161
email templates, 61
employing others
  as a path for growth, 52–53
  planning for, 58–64
entrepreneur role, 56
entrepreneurial spirit, 1, 17, 54
entry barriers, 35
environment, analysing trends, 36
equity finance, 74
Excel. *See also* templates
  AutoSum formula, 112
  checking for accuracy, 163
  how-to videos, 120
  linking worksheets, 122
  relationships between
    expenses, 115
exchange rates, 36, 95
exclusive distribution, 20
exit barriers, 35
exit plans, 63, 166
expansion. *See* growing your
    business
expenses
  10 per cent rule, 115
  at start-up, 69
  checking against goals, 164
  forecasting, 107–118

irregular, 115
  paid from personal funds, 69
  Profit & Loss Projection, 123
  reducing, 72
  relationships between, 115
  start-up, 67
  versus assets, 67
export costs, 95
exporting budgets from accounting
    software, 113

• F •

family
  balancing commitments, 51
  borrowing from, 75
  importance of involving, 9
  offering home as equity, 74
family home, borrowing against, 74
feasibility studies, 137
Ferriss, Timothy, 62
figures, double-checking, 163
finance
  applying for, 155
  debt, 74
  equity, 74
  loans and leases, 73
financial planning cycle, 15
financial projections
  checking, 163
  how far to go, 15
  how long they take, 14
  presenting in your plan, 154
  what to include, 14
financial reports, what to include in
    your plan, 12, 148, 149
fixed expenses,
  defined, 92
  versus variable costs, 94, 109
forecasting
  expenses, 107–118
  sales, 86–89
franchises
  and image management, 136
  as a goal, 50

franchises *(continued)*
  benefits of, 60
  creating your own, 56
  defined, 54
  using for inspiration, 62
future competitor, 35–36

• *G* •

Gerber, Michael, 56
getting help, 9
goals
  checking against financials,
    163
  quantifying, 159
  setting, 62, 126, 138–140
  SMART, 139, 158
  translating into action, 158
  versus objectives, 158
Godin, Seth, 34
government legislation
  analysing impact of, 37
  impact of changes, 43
green trends, 44
gross profit
  calculating, 97–102
  defined, 127
  per hour, 103
  per unit, 104
  understanding, 105
Gross Profit Projections
  as part of Profit & Loss, 121
  checking, 126
  creating, 91–105
  for many products, 105
growing your business
  building a vision, 55
  building systems, 60
  by employing others, 53
  deciding if you want to, 50–51
  limitations, 53, 63
GST
  in sales forecasts, 88
  including in expenses, 117
  start-up expenses, 67

• *H* •

hats, wearing different ones, 58
head-to-head competitors, 31–32
holidays, allowing for, 84, 115
hourly charge-out rate, 100
how-to Excel videos, 120
hybrid pricing, 80, 81

• *I* •

ideas, generating, 26
identifying variable costs
    checklist, 93
image, building, 61, 135–136
income, measuring, 63
incoming costs, 94
indirect costs. *See* fixed expenses
industries in decline, 37
industry analysis
  backing up assumptions, 165
  how often to update, 13
  how to do it, 36–38
  trends, 36–37
  where to include in your
    plan, 163
  worksheet, 37
industry benchmarks, 89
inspiration, sparking, 164, 166
intellectual property, strategic
    advantage, 20
interest, showing on financials, 117
inventory
  budgeting for at start-up,
    66–67
  calculating margins on, 100–101
investors, recommended plan
    structure, 8
irregular payments, 115

• *J* •

job costing, 62, 96, 97, 101, 104
Jobs, Steve, 23

• *K* •

keywords, 145–146
KPIs, sales, 139

• *L* •

labour
  allocating to roles, 56–60
  budgeting for, 89
  valuing, 97
leases, 72–73
legal advice, and your business
    plan, 9
life cycle of a business, 36
lifestyle issues, 43, 50–52, 64
limitations to growth, 63
line of credit, 73
linking worksheets, 122
liveplan.com, 10
living expenses, 65, 69
loans. *See also* finance
  affordability of, 71
  security against, 74
  showing on projections, 117,
    130, 156
loyalty schemes, 82, 145

• *M* •

manager role, 56
manufacturing
  costings, 96
  custom product, 97
  gross margins, 101
  Gross Profit Projection, 104
  procedures, 61
  start-up budget, 66
  variable costs, 92
margins. *See* gross profit; net profit
market research, 89, 137
market segments, 86
marketing budgets
  allocating, 142
  matching with financials, 158

marketing plans
  allocating time for, 14
  competitive analysis, 138
  market research, 137
  sales strategies, 140
  structure of, 134
  what to include, 158
MAUS MasterPlan, 10
milestones, setting, 159
mission statements, 12, 149,
    151–152
monthly expenses, 112, 115
moving annual turnover
    analysis, 150
multi-level pricing, 83

• *N* •

net profit
  calculating, 125
  deciding what's reasonable, 127
  defined, 127
niche business, 16
niche strategy, 34
no-frills pricing, 80
non-financial performance
    measures, 138, 145

• *O* •

objectives
  costing, 164
  defined, 158
  setting, 140
  summarising, 150
  versus goals, 158
offshoring of labour, 36
one-off expenses. *See* start-up
    expenses
online performance, 145
online resources, 9
operating expense versus start-up
    expense, 70, 71
operational plans, 35, 95, 148,
    150, 157

opportunities
  analysing, 42–45
  exploiting, 46
outgoing costs, 95
overheads. *See* fixed expenses
owner-operator businesses, 51
owners' salaries, budgeting for,
  69, 118

● *P* ●

package pricing, 81
Paste Link command, 121, 122, 124
people planning, 13, 58–64, 156
performance measures, 138, 145
performance objectives. *See*
  objectives
personal expenses
  budgeting for, 65, 69, 107, 118
  showing on projections, 130
  worksheet, 118
personal funds used for
  start-up, 69
personal life, managing, 43
personal tax, 116
phone scripts, 61
plan of action, 48
PlanHQ.com, 10
point of difference
  articulating, 135
  as a strategy, 33
premium pricing, 80
pricing
  monitoring, 83
  standardising, 62
pricing strategies
  as a strategic advantage, 23
  competitors, 28
  cost leadership, 33
  understanding, 77–83
procedures, developing, 61
product branding, 135
product costings. *See* costs
production labour, 92, 101
production plan, 157

profit. *See also* gross profit;
  net profit
  versus cash, 130
Profit & Loss Projections
  checking, 163
  checklist, 126
  expenses, 123
  forecasting sales, 120
  format of, 124
  how to create, 119–131
  how often to update, 14
  showing start-up expenses, 71
  variable costs, 122
  versus Cashflow Projection,
    129
  what expenses to include, 109
  what if scenarios, 54
profitability, analysing, 71, 100,
    127, 144
projects, costing, 101
psychographic analysis, 137

● *Q* ●

quantity-break pricing, 82

● *R* ●

rank, analysing, 145
raw materials, 67, 92, 93
referral sources, tracking, 144
relationships, safeguarding, 75
renting equipment, 72
repairs and maintenance, 70
repayments. *See* loans
resource requirements
  equipment, 73
  finance, 65–75
  people, 9, 49–64
retailers
  start-up budget, 66
  variable costs, 92
risk
  assessing, 128
  comfort factor, 129

planning for, 13, 150, 153, 158
versus gain, 21
roles, defining, 56, 156

• S •

sales forecasts
creating, 86–89, 105
templates, 87, 88, 104
sales strategies
establishing, 139
evaluating, 140–143
sales targets
breaking into detail, 138
setting goals, 138–140, 142
versus actuals, 144
sales tax
in sales forecasts, 88
including in expenses, 117
start-up expenses, 67
scenario analysis
how to do it, 129
long-term growth, 54
when to include, 155
scorecards
business model, 16–18
business performance, 41
competitors, 33
strategic advantage, 22–23
seasonal variations, 87, 115
security (on loans), 72, 74
self-employment, benefits of, 51
selling your business, 166
service business
costing your service, 94
Gross Profit Projection, 103
pricing your service, 81
template for, 103
variable costs, 92, 99
shipping costs, 93
skills, rating your own, 42
SMART (goals), 139, 143
specialist advice, 165
staffing requirements, 13,
58–64, 156

stakeholders
customising your plan for, 156
finance options, 72
start-up expenses
budgeting for, 65–75
defined, 70
reducing, 72
versus operating expense,
70–71, 108
worksheet, 67
stock
budgeting for at start-up,
66–67
calculating margins on,
100–101
strategic advantage
examples of, 20–21
generating ideas for, 22, 26
growing over time, 25
key attributes, 22
pricing, 23
retailers, 20
and risk, 21
scorecard, 23
statement of, 24
summarising, 149, 161
versus competitive strategy, 34
versus Unique Selling Point, 135
strengths
analysing, 40–42, 45
developing strategies for, 47
exploiting, 164
structure of written plan, 148
subcontract labour, 92, 93, 100
success, analysing, 59, 63
sustainable growth, 72
SWOT analysis, 13, 39, 45–48, 150, 158
synergy, example of, 25
systems, evaluating, 143

• T •

target market
channel analysis, 137
defining, 134, 136

taxes
  on financial projections, 126
  planning for, 116, 125
technician role, 56
technological change, 36–37, 43
templates
  Bplans, 10
  business expenses, 109–112
  Cashflow Projections, 131
  competitor analysis, 32
  customer analysis, 137
  for emails, 61
  for this book, 3, 9
  manufacturers, 104
  personal expenses, 118
  risk management, 154
  Sales Forecast worksheet, 88–89
  scenario analysis, 129
  service businesses, 103
  SWOT analysis, 45
  versus planning software, 10
The 4-Hour Workweek, 62
The E-Myth, 56
threats, guarding against, 46
time frames, managing, 11, 48, 140,
  158, 164
top ten sales strategies, 140
trends, industry analysis, 37

• *U* •

under-capitalisation, 70
Unique Selling Point, 135
unit costings, 104

• *V* •

value-based pricing, 79, 80
values statement, 149
variable costs
  identifying, 93
  modelling, 105
  percentage of sales, 105
  Profit & Loss Projection, 122
  service businesses, 94, 100
  understanding, 92–93
  versus fixed expenses, 94, 109
variances, analysing, 143, 159
VAT
  in sales forecasts, 88
  including in expenses, 117
  start-up expenses, 67
veechicurtis.com.au, 3
videos
  Cashflow Projection, 131
  Excel how-to, 120
  scenario analysis, 129
vision (for your business)
  creating, 49–64
  nurturing, 1, 164, 166
  statements of, 152

• *W* •

wages
  budgeting for, 115
  on costs, 115
  on Profit & Loss Projection, 128
Watson, Don, 151
weaknesses, analysing, 40–42
websites
  analysing traffic, 146
  for this book, 3
wholesalers, start-up budget, 66
working capital
  ensuring you have enough, 70
  preserving, 72, 73, 82
working week, 84–85
work–life balance, 43
worksheets
  business expenses, 109–112
  business performance, 41
  Cashflow Projection, 131
  Industry Analysis, 37
  linking, 122
  personal expenses, 118
  sales forecasts, 88–89
  scenario analysis, 129
  service businesses, 103
Wozniak, Steve, 23